# Faith and Forest

## by Ron Puettmann

# REFLECTING IN NATURE,
# INSPIRED BY FAITH

# Faith and Forest

by Ron Puettmann

# Reflecting in Nature,

# Inspired by Faith

ISBN: 1-4107-9300-1 (e-book)
ISBN: 1-4107-9299-4 (Paperback)

This book is printed on acid free paper.

Scripture taken from the HOLY BIBLE, NEW INTERNATIONAL VERSION®. Copyright © 1973, 1978, 1984 by International Bible Society. Uses by permission of International Bible Society.

1stBooks – rev. 11/25/03

# † Acknowledgement

This book is for You, my Lord. I hope and pray that these nets will harvest a magnificent catch for Your kingdom.

This book is also for you mom and dad. Ever since I was a young boy, I somehow knew your love of God, family and nature would give my life direction. Thank you for introducing me to God, and for teaching me the way of the cross. The Lord is my Almighty Savior, and without God in my life, I would not have the joy and peace I have come to know.

My love and respect for you is greater than the mightiest oak; it overflows the bounds of my heart. May God bless you both and may His face always shine upon you.

# † Contents

†

# Foreword

**"This is what the Lord, the God of Israel, says: 'Write in a book all the words I have spoken to you...'" (Jeremiah 30:2)**

Has there ever been a time in your life when you just couldn't help but remark at the natural beauty around you? Was it a spectacular sunset, where blue skies melted into grays, and gray skies washed into yellows, and finally, yellow skies blossomed into a seemingly endless orange horizon? Perhaps, was it a breathtakingly crisp autumn morning, where you witnessed a magnificent whitetail deer under a sentry red oak amongst frost-covered leaves and a blanket of acorns? By any chance, did you happen to be sitting along the lake's edge and witness a regal pair of wood ducks as their whistling flight ended in the timbered bay where you watched?

For some of us, natural splendors are witnessed every single day, occurrences for which certain eyes keep vigilant watch. For others, the uplifting spiritual revelations of nature only occur when troubled lives turn to the Lord in simpler, less complicated places.

This earth possesses many of these simpler, sacred places of solace. My favorite will always remain the old apple tree in Tillie's woods. A short, but bushy tree, it produced some of the juiciest green apples I have ever tasted. I remember how it sat in a pastured portion of the woods, among gooseberry bushes and oak trees. It was a spot where my dad and I would stop from squirrel hunting to rest a spell and enjoy some of God's fruit. I will always remember this as our spot, one under blue skies with billowy white clouds, filled with sounds of woodpeckers and chattering squirrels. Nothing will diminish this place in my mind, even a trip back to it years later with my dad. The knees weren't getting along as well as they used to, dad had said, but when we managed to make our way to that old apple tree, we found it dead and fallen. It was disheartening in a way, but reality in another. That apple tree, even though long gone, still holds so many great memories of my childhood spent with my father, and it always will.

There are countless other places I fondly reminisce about, and yearn to experience again. For as many secluded locations as I have found to enjoy nature and contemplate my life, there are thousands more undiscovered and awaiting the opportunity to be fully appreciated by another.

For the short time I have been here on this earth, the Lord has blessed me tremendously. One gift I am especially grateful for is nature. God has allowed nature to be an integral part of each year of my life. God has also granted me complete use of my senses, enabling me to fully appreciate the wonders of nature I see each day. Growing up on a farm with a family who relied on the outdoors for sustenance, I was given daily opportunities to experience nature. Some days it was working in the fields, other days it was hunting in the forests.

From gardening to planting trees to trapping pocket gophers, the outdoors has always been near and dear to my heart. Following my heart has led me to pursue a career with the Iowa Department of Natural Resources. Here I have found rewarding work protecting and enhancing our natural resources as a park manager within the state parks system. I have found my work to be more meaningful with each year that has passed.

Having given you a little of my background, I must tell you that the pressing motivation behind this book is the power of the Holy Spirit, and how God has been changing my life over the course of this past year. I want to express to everybody who would read my words the joy I have found in knowing Jesus Christ. With Christ as the guiding force in my life, it is impossible for me to keep the Lord's love and grace bottled up inside.

At the same time I want to urge my readers to experience our natural world, a place I hold as sacred space, a place where God is always near to me, somewhere created for reflection and prayer. I have spent practically all of my life among nature exploring, playing, learning, working and relaxing. Our natural world is a place where I can find solitude from the stresses of life and fully sense the loving arms of our Almighty Creator. My hope is to give you a sense of the joy I have found in God and nature.

My purpose in this writing is not to judge the merits of any particular interest in the outdoors. Lines will always be drawn between different issues. It is not my place to judge either side.  In our lives, we as humans are compelled to follow convictions that we hold most dear to our hearts. Right or wrong in God's eyes is my only concern.  I firmly believe our Lord has called me to share this writing with you.  In this book, I will occasionally refer to God as "He," "Him" or "Father."  This is the way I have been taught to talk about God since I was young.  These references are quite simply years of personal religious traditions and beliefs that came forth in my writing.

For a long time, God has been telling me to write.  Over the years, I have done a lot of writing, but I haven't done it for God.  I hadn't been listening. I didn't realize the journey God had in store for me.

We all have a journey in life and we all have a purpose. Some of us find out earlier than others what that purpose is. Whether it is sooner or later does not matter, only that we are able to make the discovery.  What is God's calling in your life?  What is the Lord's purpose for you?  The calling I have heard ever since I was a child was to work with God's creation in nature.  To this day, I still feel driven to protect and enhance our natural resources.  Over the past year, however, I have come to sense God urging me to do more.  This book, which I originally started in 1999 as a piece about experiencing our natural environment, fizzled after about ten pages.  In the fall of 2002, while attending a retreat sponsored by the United Methodist Church in Solon, Iowa, I felt someone tugging at my shirtsleeve.  I looked to see who it was, and I found God there by my side.  I have not turned back.  And so, with the Lord's help and the support of a loving, devoted and encouraging wife, I have written my first book.

Faith and Forest is my attempt to help you seek natural places of solace and to promote developing a stronger relationship with Jesus Christ through reflection.  I intend to show our natural world through the eyes of a common man to encourage spiritual growth.

My mind has taken me back both to days of my youth and of those days not long ago, remembering moments in my life which stood out as signs of God's presence.

As you read the stories and chapters ahead, open your mind and your heart to the possibilities in God's realm.  Be willing to listen for God's voice in your life.  The Lord does have big plans for each and every one of us, even when obstinate heads and hearts are prone to believe otherwise.

If what is written on these pages encourages even one person to seek God and nature on a higher level, then it has been successful in my mind.

I am a firm believer that prayer before every task I undertake helps deepen my faith with God. Even short prayers open my heart to God's will and prepare me to accept whatever may happen in my daily life. And so, as you press forward with this book, I have written a short prayer to begin your journey:

Dear Lord,

You know my heart and everything about me.

I ask that You be with me this day.

Open my heart to Your will.

Guide me, that I may realize Your purpose for my life.

Amen.

**"I press on toward the goal to win the prize for which God has called me heavenward in Christ Jesus." (Philippians 3:14)**

# † Part I

## Forest

**"Then all of the trees of the forest will sing for joy." (Psalms 96:12)**

I have heard it said that being close to nature is being close to God. I believe this to be true. Whether you are an avid outdoorsman or environmentalist, mushroom hunter or mountain climber, birdwatcher or botanist, nature holds one common, uniting bond with all people. Nature is God's magnificent creation, worthy of admiration and respect. It is awe-inspiring, often times breathtaking, and is a place God created for us to reflect and worship.

Natural "getaways" do not have to be twenty miles from the nearest road. They can be found in a marsh just across the section from a major highway, within the timbered confines of the busiest state parks in Iowa, or even in the shallow ravine which separates your lot from the neighbors, one hundred feet away.

I have found nature to be absolutely filled with sacred spaces, areas of solitude where God calls me to conversation. Would you care to join me?

✝

# Chapter 1

## Reflect

**"May my meditation be pleasing to him, as I rejoice in the Lord." (Psalm 104:34)**

For each one of us, our journey to find God is different. Some find God as a child and live a full, devoted life, praising the Lord's name. Others come to know the Lord in their last moments of life on earth and are saved. Most find God somewhere in between as they search for answers in life, an existence that is quite often hard to understand.

Where we find God is as different as when we find Him. I have found God in many ways. First, I have found our Lord in all things natural, in all of creation. I see our Almighty Creator with the changing of each season. In spring I see God as flowers shoot forth from rain-dampened soils and as a seemingly lifeless landscape transforms daily into a living mosaic filled with color, vitality and all manner

3

of plants and creatures.  In summer I see God as whitetail fawns gain confidence walking on new developing legs and as red-winged blackbirds and meadowlarks raise their young and teach them to fly.  In autumn I find the Lord in the spectacular array of changing colors before trees begin to lose their leaves, and I see God in the multitudes of migrating waterfowl.  In winter I see our Father in soft, gentle snowfalls, long icicles, and in the January thaw we are blessed with each year.

I see Him in the starry heavens, in peaceful rainfalls, in billowy clouds.  To me, God is in the black cherry tree, the tallgrass prairie, the hazelnut and the redbud.  God can be seen in the shimmering waters of easy-flowing creeks, in the mirror reflection of a calm lake and in the smallest of puddles.  I witness God as a red-tailed hawk alights on a tree branch, as a chipmunk scurries busily across the forest floor, as a great blue heron wades in shallow waters in search of food, and in the dazzling movements of a ruby-throated hummingbird.  God's presence is evident to me in the harmonious chorus of spring peepers, in the shrill cry of a screech owl, in the excited yips and yelps of coyotes on a cold winter's night and in the silence of the forest on a September morning.

After coming to find and know the Lord in the glorious creation that surrounds me, I have also found God in everyday events and through people I meet. I have come to believe that God works through each one of us, giving us the opportunity to show love by our every action, word and thought. I have come to see God's love in the friendly wave of a stranger while driving in the car, and in the simple, yet kind gestures people show to each other every day. Perhaps it is holding the door open for somebody behind you as you enter the convenience store. Maybe it is allowing somebody else to proceed ahead of you at a four-way stop when you happen to stop at the same time. I have even found our Lord in more obvious ways, like the bumper sticker my niece Michelle has on her car that reads, "Are You Following God This Closely?"

God is in our service to friends and strangers, in our gifts to those in need and in our sympathy cards to people we don't even know.

I have seen God working through people in unique and inspiring ways, and have felt His presence in my life over and over again. Jesus has promised that he will always be with us. In Hebrews 13:5, scripture reads, "…'Never will I leave you; Never will I forsake you.'" I have found this to be true in each year of my life. Jesus is with me through the hardest of times and the best of times. In an average, ordinary day, Christ walks beside me with each step that I take. If I allow my heart to notice, I see and hear our Lord all around me. As my heart feels Christ's presence, I realize that all of my cares, concerns and worries melt away. His companionship gives me a constant source of peace and assurance.

Do you have a place to reflect? If so, where is it that you find solace and comfort? For many people, the church building is that quiet place where they can go every day to talk to God. But for most people in today's society, this isn't the case. I have seen and heard people say that their vehicle is that place of reflection. Once they close the door, they can tune out life and concentrate on talking with God. When it is raining or windy outside, it is dry and comfortable inside. Once they are done praying, they turn on Christian music and continue to praise God through song.

The power of song is an amazing thing. Songs can take you back, in an instant, to some of your earliest memories. They can make you laugh and they most assuredly can make you cry. Listening carefully to the words of Christian songs, I have often times been brought to tears—mostly tears of joy—by how their meaning had grabbed my heart. The Good News of Jesus Christ is brought to listeners in a powerful and joyful way.

Getting back to the car, I find that I am able to spend quality time with the Lord when driving. Throughout my daily job duties, I am often so preoccupied with busy work that I only find time for quick prayers of thanks or simple prayers for help. However, because of the nature of my work, I am afforded numerous five to ten-minute trips in the vehicle each day. These are fantastic opportunities for me to pray and hear more about God's message through music or Christian programming.

While the vehicle is a great place of comfort and prayer, I would say hands down that being outdoors, especially in the forest, is where I find my daily sanctuary, my place of reflection and refuge. Now, the church sanctuary will always be my formal place of worship. I thoroughly enjoy fellowship with other members of the congregation and find worship times more meaningful spiritually every week. I find great comfort and peace in my service to the church, which continues to grow. But the church sanctuary cannot *physically* be my daily and even hourly place of reflection and prayer. I must go to the sanctuary *spiritually* in other ways throughout each day. For me, that primary way is by means of God's creation in the outdoors.

When I am in the forest, my soul is elevated to another level. I can lift up my problems, my fears, my concerns and any number of prayers in a way I find difficult or impossible when surrounded by the distractions of life.

Even in the vehicle, I must focus on driving and those around me. In the forest, my surroundings help me to focus, rather than distract me. Each tree and plant I see, every sound I hear, and each creature I witness moving about reminds me of God's presence. These sights and sounds heighten my spiritual awareness and allow my time of reflection to be truly meaningful.

# God Calls us to Reflect

Isn't God's creation awesome and grand in its entire splendor? I believe there are many reasons God made it this way. Our loving God created us in His image and wanted us to have a special place to live. The Lord created forests, prairies, rivers, mountains, and countless wild places, each with its own breathtaking beauty and unique qualities. I believe God gave these places to us for two reasons. First, God wants us to use our natural resources wisely and be good stewards of all that was created. Second, God calls us to use this magnificent creation for worship and praise. God wants us to give our love and praises back to Him.

I don't believe God meant for us to be irresponsible with the gifts we have been given. Responsible stewardship involves wisely using and conserving these natural resources. For every tree harvested for our use, I think God would want us to plant two more to replace it, thus ensuring that our Lord's creation will continue for future generations. This is my personal feeling, a reflection passed onto me by my father, and it is one I believe to be in the Lord's keeping. It is because of this philosophy that I find so much enjoyment working with natural resources, particularly forests and prairies.

God also calls us to use these jewels of creation to reflect on the teachings of Jesus Christ and his word. God wants us to set aside quiet time for ourselves in forests to ponder His will in our lives. God wants us to take slow walks through prairies to lift up our concerns and deepen our faith. God made the sound of a shallow stream just as it is, so that we may sit next to it with our back against the bole of a leafy giant and feel the Lord's peace surround us.

# Snap of the Lord's Fingers

Every so often, I witness the snap of God's fingers. The thought of this makes me smile with the widest of smiles. God snaps His fingers and suddenly I hear a tree fall down in the forest. Thunderous snapping and crackling sounds reverberate through the timber as I look to see a mighty oak tree take several smaller trees with it in its incredible descent. Immediately I think to myself, "Lord you are magnificent!" (And I also think to myself that if a tree fell in the forest and nobody was around to hear it that it would *indeed* make a sound!).

Sometimes the snap of our Lord's fingers isn't so dramatic. Once it was the small branch of a juniper bush suddenly springing up out of a snow bank as the springtime sun melted the snow away. Late one evening it was the sharp smack of a beaver's tail on the water abruptly opening my heavy eyelids as I fished from the lakeshore.

Sometimes in early spring as I stand down along the river, God snaps those beautiful, mighty fingers and an enormous chunk of ice breaks loose and flows downstream.

I can only marvel at the natural processes God has created, processes I and countless others will never fully understand. Butterflies landing on your jacket, stars streaking across the evening sky, rain showers during sunny weather that only last a few seconds, a hickory nut falling out of the tree above you and landing on the book that you are reading, witnessing a hawk swoop down on a field mouse in the ditch the instant that you pass by in your vehicle. Processes and events that may seem insignificant to some are absolute signs of God's constant presence to me.

One warm, sunny April afternoon the fabulous spring weather changed to gray and bitterly cold in the matter of a couple hours. It appeared that the conditions might produce some snow. Always concerned with driving in wet, heavy snow, I thought to myself, "It will take a pretty good-sized storm before these roads get too bad, given the temperature." I only had an hour before my workday was finished. Not five minutes after this thought, as I pulled the vehicle into the parking lot, I noticed the light pelting of pea-sized hail on the cab and hood of my work truck. I walked quickly from the vehicle to the shop, closed the door behind me and then just watched. Within moments, the entire world immediately outside was blanketed with small beads of ice. I recalled my thoughts, not five minutes earlier, then apologized to the Lord for doubting His power. I had temporarily forgotten who was in charge. With a snap of the Lord's fingers, God sent down a springtime hailstorm that quickly reminded me of His majestic and awesome power.

# Hear the Lord Speak

Has God ever talked to you? I think most people would say "No." But in reply, how do you know? I believe that I hear God's voice every single day. Each time the wind blows I hear those soft whispers from our heavenly God. Even as the sun rises on a crisp clear winter morning, I hear those words, "I am giving you another day, make the most of it." I hear God's comforting voice in a mourning dove's lonesome cry. I believe God "speaks" to us in many ways. There are only a few servants chosen throughout history that God has physically spoken to. For the rest of us, God sends messages in other ways. Nature is where I hear our Creator's voice the most. When cardinals sing, God subtly reminds me that life is a vibrant blessing and I need to give Him thanks. And so I do. "Thank you Lord for this day, and the opportunity to appreciate this moment."

Occasionally I take our family dog, Tigger, for a walk down along the lakeshore early in the morning as I make time to pray to the Lord. As the dark skies lighten with the coming of dawn, a wild turkey gobbles from across the lake, its call echoing through the timbered hillsides around me. In that moment I hear God challenging me, that our Lord is bringing the world a new day and is giving me another chance to be His faithful follower. "Shout to the world the Good News of the Lord!" I hear, as God reminds me that one of my daily missions needs to be to enlarge His kingdom.

One such morning, I heard a barred owl, Canada goose, mallard duck, wild turkey, rooster pheasant, nighthawk, mourning dove, cardinal, crow, robin and several other songbirds I couldn't recognize by their sound. The Lord was most certainly talking with me that morning!

Most mornings in the summer, as I finish my prayer time, I hear a multitude of robins chirping in that final hour around sunrise. But I don't hear robins alone, I hear a joyful message from God in addition. The Lord tells me that each day should start with a song, and that music should last the entire day right there in my heart.

"It is good to praise the Lord and make music to Your name, O Most High." (Psalm 92:1)

My workday starts, and quite often, as I am out and about, squirrels bark and chatter among leafy branches. I hear God's voice calling me to remember the teachings of Jesus Christ, and God tells me to serve others as I go through the day. Chipmunks scurry across the forest floor and God urges me to stay industrious in my duties. Crows raucous calls, though annoying to some, are God's words too. With each note they remind me that Jesus died on a cross for my sins, and I need to keep this fact in mind. Occasionally, I cross a small creek. Water flowing over rocky shallows gurgles a pleasant tune. This is the Lord telling me I have peace in my life, and I should pass this peace on to others. As low breezes scatter forest leaves, I hear God whisper, "Follow me." Sometimes during a light rain, I can hear the prayers of Jesus in the garden, "Not Mine, but Your will be done."

After heavy snowfalls, I see pine trees blanketed and covered in white with tracks of deer and fox meandering throughout. I am often the first person to see these areas blanketed with new-fallen snow. Each time I hear God say, "See My glory," and at these times I give our Lord thanks for a beauty unmatched by human hands. Many times, I've walked across an iced-covered lake, and it still amazes me to hear the resonating cracks and pops as I pass over the top. The sounds are quite unique, starting directly beneath you and reverberating in all directions, almost like a spider's web. I hear God say, "Tread lightly."

Thus far, God's messages I described have been rather subtle. Occasionally the Lord's words are much more dramatic and direct. One tumultuous thunderstorm that I experienced at Iowa's Ledges (described in a later chapter) sealed my decision to pursue a career with state parks. This storm is one example of how God can speak to us rather loudly. That day, I heard God say, "This is the road I want you to take. I have a purpose for you somewhere down this road, so don't stray from the path."

Tornadoes, hurricanes, volcanic eruptions, earthquakes, damaging hail, torrential rains and flooding are all examples of God's direct instructions. At these times, God shouts, "Don't forget who gave you what you have!" For what God has so generously given to us can also be taken away. So we give thanks to the Lord for sparing us from the storm. We give thanks to God for giving us direction. We thank our Lord for life. And then something amazing and miraculous occurs. The sun shines out from behind dark, ominous clouds and sends forth glorious rays of brilliant light. God tells us that we are forgiven and once again we will be given another chance.

Although I try not to, I am certain there are days when I take God's creation in nature for granted. I also take for granted the senses God has given me to appreciate these wonders. Whatever your level may be in experiencing the outdoor world, open your mind and heart to the possibilities when God takes you by the hand and leads the way.

"By faith we understand that the universe was formed at God's command..." (Hebrews 11:3)

# God in Nature

For me, finding God in nature is an everyday occurrence. I see God's grand design each time that I see a kestrel alight upon a lofty perch. Each time I watch the leaves of a quaking aspen tree shimmering in the breeze, I can sense God's hand at work.

I have a love for windy, brushy creek bottoms. Perhaps you have seen one, the kind that meanders through crop fields like an eerie looking snake, with the occasional oak tree giving it the appearance of a great hideout for that solitary buck you have only seen in magazines or on television. The kind of creek bottom with just enough creek to make it a raccoon or mink haven. The kind where water always flows, but in such small amounts that crossing the creek requires only an effortless jump. God is in this kind of place. Although they seem to be less traveled, brushy creek bottoms are wild places too, filled with signs of the Lord's presence.

I have long enjoyed walking through an autumn field of switchgrass with outspread hands brushing across the tops.

Each time I do, I get the sense that I am brushing my hands along the glorious cloak of Jesus Christ.

Sometimes the Lord shows me His works in dramatic ways. In late autumn while hunting, I walk through the forest. The crunching of dry leaves under my feet makes it virtually impossible to sneak up on any animal. All of the sudden, an elusive ruffed grouse explodes skyward, dodging countless branches, as I sneak through dense groves of aspen and birch with gooseberries tugging at my cuffs.

In less dramatic ways, God can be seen in the simple wonders of nature. On a windy day when overlooking a tallgrass prairie, I watch as the grasses sway back and forth, almost like waves in the ocean. I envision God's hands lightly passing over them as each wave goes by. My soul marvels at trees, how tall and massive they can become, and how strong they are. I like to compare a sentinel oak tree with a life of faith…

The oak tree has deep roots grounded in faith, which constantly reach for spiritual waters. It's powerful, thick trunk is able to withstand the storms of temptation, hatred and discrimination. Strong branches continually reach for

God's heavenly kingdom. And although storms of sin may come and break branches, with roots deep in faith, it cannot be uprooted from a strong relationship with Christ.

O Lord, help my faith to be like this oak tree.

"God saw all that he had made, and it was very good..." (Genesis 1:31)

†

# Chapter 2

# Early Accounts

"As the deer pants for streams of water, so my soul pants for you, O God. My soul thirsts for God, for the living God..." (Psalms 42:1-2)

## To Be 16 Again...

The northern Iowa temperature was quite brisk that early November morning. Trapping season had just begun, and I was making a raccoon set near a culvert across from my father's fields. In the southeastern sky, a spectacular orange sun rose slightly above the horizon, and its image reflected from one of many ponds, which naturally occupied the fields. I bent over, reached down in the icy cold water and picked up my trap to set it. And then I heard them. What began as light and distant echoes, soon turned into the vibrant, proud calls of a flock of Canada geese. I felt the cold November breeze strike my bare lower back as I was stooped over. The Canada's honking grew louder, and soon I recognized the sounds for what they were. I stood up slowly and watched. A dozen large geese in their ancestral "v" formation flew directly over my head, not more than twenty feet above. They slowed up at our pond and circled as if they needed a rest from their long flight. I was in for no such treat. The geese caught sight of me standing there, not fifty yards away, and decided that there were safer havens to be found.

I must have been about sixteen or so at the time, so it has been many years since this scene transpired in my life, yet it is one I will never forget. This event and many like it are what shaped and molded me into the person I am today. My passion for our natural world would not be as strong if it weren't for two factors: growing up with a family who enjoyed the outdoors, and finding God in all natural things.

# Iowa's Ledges

I am in recollection of my first season working as a natural resource aide for the Iowa Department of Natural Resources at Ledges State Park near Boone. I was given numerous duties, one of which was mowing "the bottom." This is a very large grassy field and picnic area located on the lower side of the park in the flood plain of the Des Moines River. As I was running the 1960's vintage tractor, I was blessed with one of those "outdoor miracles." Thunderclouds began to roll in from the west, blanketing the sky. The lower Ledges, which in this particular area is wide open, transformed before my eyes from a picturesque July afternoon to an ominous, threatening wall of storm clouds. Marching like a battalion of soldiers, this storm charged into battle. As the winds picked up, I could just feel the clouds ready to unload massive amounts of rainwater to the earth. Fortunately that same sense of rain also directed me to shelter, for as soon as I reached it, the skies let loose and the rains fell. Never can I remember the feeling of an approaching storm like I felt in the air around me that day at Iowa's Ledges.

I am a firm believer in the philosophy that God directs my life. God's will guides me to where He wants me to be at any given point in time. Even if where I am doesn't seem to be a good fit, God has plans for me in that place. When the Lord's will has been accomplished, God will let me know that it is time to move on. I have been working for the Department now for just under ten years. Each and every position I have ever held to get to where I am now has truly been the grace of God. Each position, including this very first one at Ledges, fell into place at exactly the right time…the Lord's time, not mine. It was not coincidence, circumstance, nor was it good luck. It was God's will.

"In his heart a man plans his course, but the Lord determines his steps." (Proverbs 16:9)

# Getting Your Hands Dirty

"Here's one." Trapper said, as the long steel rod descended effortlessly into the soil beneath his weight. Referring to the pocket gopher's underground tunnel that he had found, he motioned for me to grab the trowel. Handing it to my brother, I watched as he did his magic. "You can't be a trapper if you don't get your hands dirty," he said, scooping out handfuls of dirt. I watched as he carefully dug downward, locating the tunnel and showing me the "Y." This was the intersection to the gopher's main tunnel. Gary, nicknamed "Trapper" in his military years, completed the set and allowed me to make the second one. The next morning, much to my delight we had caught the rodent making a mess of our driveway.

My brother taught me a couple of life-long lessons that day: 1) If you want to succeed at a task, take the time and effort to do your best job; and 2) Don't be afraid to get your hands dirty. Gary also brought me a lot closer to the outdoors, for which I am incredibly thankful. I couldn't have been much more than seven years old at the time, but I remember it like it was yesterday. Not many years later I was trapping alongside Gary and two more brothers, Phil and Brian, learning more about wild animals then I could ever have imagined.

After looking back on that incident I have come to realize that my Christian life needs to follow those two lessons my brother taught me. Everything I do should be done with a conscientious mind, willing heart and determined hands. And just like on that day, I can't be afraid to get my hands dirty. Another way to phrase it would be, don't be afraid to get your feet wet. I am only beginning to learn and carry out the different ways God is asking me to honor Him by serving others. For a long time, I have been afraid to get my hands dirty. I have been afraid to get my feet wet. Anybody who has stepped into a stream with tennis shoes on, knows about the strange feeling that occurs right away. But after only a few moments, you become accustomed to it, and soon the feeling is actually a comfortable one. And so is serving others.

I know that I have a lot of work ahead of me and much more service that I could be doing, but I also realize that

*God smiles on even the smallest of efforts.* And this encourages me to do more.

"…But as for me and my household, we will serve the Lord." (Joshua 24:15)

†

# Chapter 3

# Pastimes

"But blessed is the man who trusts in the Lord, whose confidence is in him. He will be like a tree planted by the water that sends out its roots by the stream. It does not fear when heat comes; its leaves are always green. It has no worries in a year of drought and never fails to bear fruit." (Jeremiah 17:7-8)

# Fishing

I can imagine that there are some pretty good fishing stories out there, and I'll wager that there are just as many stories about the one that got away. Most of my favorite memories come from fishing with my dad along the Little Cedar River. Dad always caught the bass, and the kids always ended up catching suckers or carp. It was great fun, however, and always an adventure to us. Although I love fishing, I cannot consider myself an avid angler. The handful of opportunities I take advantage of each year are refreshing days spent in reflection.

Fishing by boat is a great way for me to spiritually partake in this pastime. From a boat, one is obviously surrounded by water, and almost immediately that relaxing feeling comes over me. At times, I simply stare at the water, watching waves roll across the lake, becoming transfixed and almost hypnotized by their repetitious motion. Other times, I watch across the lake, noticing the timbered shorelines, sometimes witnessing whitetail deer, squirrels, wild turkeys and occasionally a red fox. I see them cautiously make their way through the forest, completely unaware of my presence.

I notice water birds, great blue and green-backed herons, wood ducks, Canada geese and scaup. Every once in a while, as I make my way into a secluded bay, the shrill cry and undulating flight of a belted kingfisher greet me. I have witnessed an osprey dive from lofty heights and descend at amazing speed into the lake. After only moments, it laboriously powered its way upward with a fish in its grasp.

At yet other times, my eyes are glued to the bobber, patiently watching and waiting. Watching and waiting. Watching for the first hint of movement like a twitch or tug. Waiting for precisely the exact moment to send the rod tip quickly upward with a snap to set the hook.

I can draw many analogies here with respect to fishing and one's faith. After all, fishing has biblical proportions and implications. In all four gospels, Jesus makes similarities between fishing and bringing people to know the Lord. Matthew 4:19 and Mark 1:17 read, "'Come, follow me,' Jesus said, 'and I will make you fishers of men.'" Luke 5:9-10 reads, "For he and all his companions were astonished at the catch of fish they had taken, and so were James and John, the sons of Zebedee, Simon's partners. Then Jesus said to Simon, 'Don't be afraid; from now on you will catch men.'" The book of John, Chapter 21 also describes the miraculous catch and Christ's request to Peter to look after His people and to follow the Messiah.

If only Christian lives might be similar in ways to fishing. If we are to be fishers of men as God would have us, we first and foremost need to get in the boat. Get on board with God. Know that Jesus Christ is our Almighty

31

Savior and succumb to His will. Accept and believe in the Lord's teachings, for they are right and pure and holy. When you fully accept the way of the cross, you have enough faith to trust God completely. If you are at this point, you are in the boat and you are on board with God.

Where I live, anglers can only use two lines at a time when fishing. This is comparable to drawing two people toward the kingdom of God at a time (when fishing is at it's best). As much as I think this will surely build up my heavenly treasures, I also feel that God wants me to do more. I think God wants me to spread out nets, spreading them out as wide as I can. If the nets don't seem to be working, I'll need to switch to the other side of the boat, even if I have already tried there. I can't be afraid to move around a bit and try different spots on the lake.

God's nets are His word. Spread the word of God as far as you can, to every one you know and those you meet. There will be times when you will have to be patient and prepared, ready to interject God's word at just the right moment. Study God's word. Study it so you can use it to expand the kingdom of our Lord. Study and know it, so that when somebody is deciding whether they should listen further or ignore your words, you can confidently use God's word for the best possible result.

Here's one fishing story for your stringer...

A bright half-moon shone clearly through an open eastern Iowa sky, and down upon the calm waters of a public lake where I was fishing. I was sitting on my old tattered lawn chair holding two long fishing poles in my lap, just enjoying the moment. All around me, thousands of fireflies silently sparkled in the darkness, shedding light on a blade of grass here, a red oak leaf there. Little brown bats cruised up and down the small trail I sat along (in fact only inches from my face at times) and out over the lake, finding an endless supply of food. In the distance, barred owls called back and forth, occasionally working themselves up into a frenzy and screaming their monkey-like calls at each other. Suddenly, there was a very large tug on my finger. I immediately extended my arm outward, allowing another two to three feet of slack in the line. As soon as I felt the line tighten, I gave a quick upward snap of the rod, and began reeling in the first of several nice channel cats that evening. I put the cat on my well-used stringer, added another crawler to the half-baited hook and cast it out again.

I leaned back again and stared up at the stars. Millions of sparkling eyes stared down from the heavens above. As I looked back down onto the lake, I noticed a beaver silently swimming by, leaving a small wake on the calm water. It slapped it's tail on the water's surface, just to remind me who's territory I was invading.

My thoughts then began drifting to that of deer hunting the hills of northeast Iowa. As I started to consider how our group could do things differently this year to outsmart the bucks, I felt another strong tug on my fingers. After setting the hook, I played this fish a little more, feeling it twist and spin in the water, something very characteristic of channel catfish. This one wasn't as large as the last, weighing only about two pounds. "Thanks, God," I said to myself.

Nights such as these were true blessings, opportunities to relax in a quiet, peaceful place. This was an opportunity to praise the Lord for such beautiful creations, and to thank Him for bringing me to this place and time. Even though I was only in the lawn chair for about two hours, the evening was full of prayer. Most were prayers of thankfulness for all of the blessings and mercy I have received in my life. Others were for family and friends and good health for them, continued enjoyment at work, upcoming events and safe travels, increased faith each day, the efforts of the church family and our pastor, and the list goes on. In simplest terms, there is no matter too small to take to the Lord in prayer.

# Bushytails

One means of happiness can be found from hearing the sounds of hickory shells dropping to the forest floor as instinct-driven fox squirrels prepare for the approaching winter season. In the upper Midwest, this is a season where only the toughest survive. A season with wind-chills and temperatures well below zero degrees, a season filled with miserably cold and frozen conditions, a season which makes it hard to imagine any animal even surviving in.

I quite clearly recall many hunts in the woods with my father. "Patience is a virtue, but only if you practice it." My dad has spoken these words to me many times. Now that I am older and have two children, dad teaches his mother's words to my two boys. I would venture to guess that squirrel hunting has to be one of life's greater teachers of patience.

On a brisk, sunny October afternoon, dad would park the truck and together we would walk to the woods. The slow walk to the woods was hard enough for me as a young boy, not even being a teenager yet. Once we reached the tree line, our movement all but stopped. My excitement reached a pinnacle at that first step into the timber. Each step after this was carefully placed and what some would consider to be painfully slow. Our eyes studied every tree for movement and shapes, as our ears tuned in to all of the forest sounds.

After walking for an hour, and perhaps only moving a hundred yards or so, we would sit in an area with a nice cluster of red oak trees. Here we would sit for half an hour, watching and listening. This had to be my favorite time, one of a pastoral, tranquil nature, where each of us took time to reflect, to pray, and often times drift off in light sleep to the sounds of the living forest around us (I'll admit that I napped anyway). After a spell, dad would give a light whistle from his position, usually about thirty to forty yards away. I would whistle back and we would continue on. Eventually our path would cross the apple tree.

Whether or not we bagged any squirrels did not matter to me. I so enjoyed the time I was able to spend with dad in the woods. Because of these times, I will forever have a special place where at any time, I can go in my mind to reflect, to pray, to regain the needed patience my dad taught me, and to feel the presence of his generous love. And in going to this place, I am able to regain focus on my life and give thanks to our heavenly Father.

Squirrel hunting and simply being in the woods have been some of my favorite opportunities for reflection. I've long enjoyed sitting in the woods, leaning up against the bole of a century-old oak tree and just listening. Listening to the scamper of little feet as squirrels meander through the leaves blanketing the forest floor, listening to their small claws scratch the trunk of a tree as they ascend to frightening heights in only moments, and listening to busy rodent teeth making short work of the season-long growth of thick walnut and hickory hulls.

Watching bushytails flicker in the bright sunlight, hearing their raucous chatter when an intruder is near, and witnessing these creatures' simple, yet industrious lives is truly one of life's more pleasurable treats.

"'You have made known to me the paths of life; you will fill me with joy in your presence.'" (Acts 2:28)

# Deer Hunts

When the Lord created all of this world's animals, God decided to make one craftier, smarter, and more elusive than most others. That animal is the whitetail deer. Have you ever hunted an animal? Specifically, have you ever hunted a whitetail buck? Simply stated, it takes intelligence and nerves of steel to perform some of the trickery that these bucks throw at today's hunters.

Many big bucks are watched all year long by avid hunters. These hunters wait all year for that big chance, but when hunting season arrives, the buck they've watched diligently all year long is nowhere to be found. What is even more frustrating is a scenario similar to this: Your hunting party knows the big buck has been seen in a 40-acre patch of timber. Your party sets up the hunt correctly, using the wind to your advantage, posting all major escape routes, and pushing the woods with an appropriate number of hunters. The hunters take their time and literally comb the woods. But wouldn't you know, Mr. Landowner (who has been watching the entire scene with a spotting scope) sees the big buck milling around and grazing on the opposite end of the woods from where the hunters end up!

Then there's the buck, which has been seen out in the middle of a section along a grassy fenceline. All of the hunters have their assigned duties, some pushing fencelines or grassy waterways a certain direction to others posting the opposite end. A hunter watching the entire ordeal observes the buck sneak out into a chisel-plowed field and lay down, virtually disappearing from view. The hunters walk past without suspecting or seeing a thing. After the hunters pass, the buck sneaks back to the fenceline and breaks out in a completely different direction, escaping for another day.

Hundreds, perhaps even thousands of stories similar to this have been told about whitetail bucks. Maybe this is one of the reasons I am drawn to the forest every year when autumn rolls around. Maybe it's the challenge of outsmarting one of these elusive and powerful creatures. But part of me thinks that it is the need to be hunting, something I absolutely love to do, with some of my closest friends.

Really, it's a fellowship of sorts. Men and women taking a few days out of their busy routines to re-unite with friends and nature. It's a fellowship that refreshes the soul; icy winds and chattering squirrels, sounds of snapping branches and a quickening pulse, finding a track and following the spoor with excited anticipation. It's a fellowship of adventure; traversing up and down steep hills and valleys, through creeks and rivers, over beaver dams, through sloughs and ditches, in and out of all kinds of timber, nearby caves, around sinkholes. All the while, you are stealthily moving, watching warily, listening alertly and hiding in anticipation of the big opportunity. The one big chance that a trophy whitetail buck will make a mistake and let itself be seen by a human at too close of a range.

It's a fellowship of friends, trusting each other with your lives. Knowing that somebody you care about is walking toward you with a loaded weapon, pushing deer directly at you, and both of you having complete confidence that neither party will fire his weapon irresponsibly.

I am absolutely certain that another reason I love hunting whitetail deer in northeast Iowa is because of the scenery. Every second or third year, our deer hunting group will take one day to hunt the hill country of Allamakee County. We are all worn out by the end of the day from going up and down those hills, but the exhaustion and sore muscles are worth it. Walking over some of the steep and rugged terrain, I have been positively convinced that I was the first person to set foot on that spot in hundreds, if not thousands of years. I try to picture who the last person was...perhaps it was an early settler moving westward, having just crossed the Mississippi River; or perhaps it was a native American several hundred years ago stalking an elk or black bear on this very spot. What a spectacular view, standing on the northeast facing slope of one of these awesome giants, somewhat near the top, watching bald eagles soaring up and down the valley. The quiet is broken only by the occasional piercing cry of the eagle, and this echoes up and down the valley like a patriotic bugle.

The scenic beauty of this area is truly awe-inspiring. For me, it is impossible to see this magnificent creation and not think of God. The Lord's hand has painted this landscape so perfectly, and I know it is one of God's many blessings bringing me back here to enjoy it. As the eagle cries up and down the valley, my heart sings out to the Lord with praise.

# Of Bows and Arrows

Somewhere along that well-traveled deer trail of my life, I was blessed with a wonderful opportunity. We all find these forks in the trail at some point in our development, and they have the potential to completely change who we are. The fork that I took began in my high school years. My older brother Phil was sitting in the office room of his fur shed talking hunting and trapping, as was the case at this time almost every evening. Phil owns a business buying, preparing and selling furs near the small north Iowa burg of Little Cedar.

Newspaper clippings, advertisements, business cards, pictures and numerous other written pieces concerning the outdoors were stapled to the walls of his office.

On this particular evening, I stopped in to talk with Phil, and the subject of bowhunting came up. I was interested in giving it a try, and wanted to ask his advice. Brother Phil had the answer, as there was an old recurve bow hanging on a gun rack in the trap room. Being the adept salesperson that he was, I became the owner of that bow five minutes and twenty dollars later.

Off and on for over ten years, I shot that bow at various targets. A couple of years, that bow only collected dust, but in other years, several rabbits fell to the somehow ancient, yet amazingly effective hunting technique. With each shot, my interest in archery grew. It was not until the sixth or seventh year of owning the bow, that I became much more interested. I finally made the time to try my hand at bowhunting whitetail deer, and all of the articles and books that I read could not compare to the actual experience. Those crisp autumn days on the deer stand have been fond memories through the winter, spring and summer months.

My first season in a bow stand brought several memorable and nostalgic moments. On that very first crisp November morning, it was not more than an hour into the hunt. There was a northwest breeze that hit my face just right and kept me alert and watchful. My first visitor was a beautiful red fox, which trotted past my stand. This specimen was in its prime, with thick, long guard hairs and a flawless brilliant red coat. In my memory, this fox was painted on a background of frost-covered field corn, ready to pick, blue November skies, and early morning sunshine on the few remaining crimson oak leaves left. My first experience with a whitetail buck came about an hour later. I was frigid to the point of chattering teeth there on stand, but loved every minute of being able to hunt with a bow. As my eyes and head slowly moved from one side of vision to the other, scanning the corn rows and timber for any movement out of the ordinary, there materialized a small 6-point buck in the corn rows to my right. He didn't come in from a distance and announce his presence, he didn't slowly and carefully sneak to this position, and he didn't bother to let me know he was coming. He was just there, all of the sudden, like an apparition, about twenty yards away. His neck was swollen and I could see breath out of his nose quite clearly. He did not see me, but of course, as soon as he arrived, he also departed, in the same mysterious direction that he had approached.

My first good chance at a young whitetail buck came several days later on a stand in a different location. My very first arrow, which likely would have pierced his heart, bounced off a tiny twig halfway to its intended target, and flew harmlessly over the buck's back. The only other opportunity that season came two days later at another young buck, who braved to walk past my stand and stop broadside at fifteen yards. My arms shook so bad, that the broadhead-tipped cedar arrow again went right over its back. I found true thrill in getting that close to a deer and having the opportunity to harvest it with a stick and string.

Seasons have come and gone since my first year pursuing whitetails in eastern Iowa. Each one has taught me more about their cunning means of survival in and around Iowa's oak-hickory woodlands, agricultural fields, and the diverse landscape around them. Each season has also raised my awareness of God's awesome creations, and has taught me to be respectful of them.

# Gardening

I love gardening. How enjoyable it is to plant a seed, prepare for that seed fertilized soil, and then sustain the developing plant with water. Fond memories bring me back to times as a young boy on the farm, following in my dad's boot prints with bare feet, as he tilled the garden. I recall my mom hoeing rows for corn and beans, then showing us how to plant the seeds. What joy it was for a young boy to do these things, and then watch as the vegetables grew. If there was any part to gardening that would keep me from ever having my own garden one day, pulling weeds was that deterrent. It must not have bothered me that badly, though, as to this day I don't seem to mind pulling weeds all that much. So many times I have sought advice from my mom and sister Kathy, who both have green thumbs. They have a love and knowledge of gardening that amazes me.

Equally satisfying to me is planting trees and watching over the years as they mature and send branches outward and upward, reaching for the heavens. It is a joy to see them house birds, squirrels and other creatures. And then as they mature, they bear fruit, which brings me delight. I sense Godly connotations in planting a garden and planting trees. Aren't we the produce of the Lord's garden? Aren't we trees in the Almighty's grand forest?

God plants each of us here on earth to grow, mature and produce fruit. How many of us become choked with weeds and the vines of sin, those unimportant parts of our lives, which deter us from true growth in the Lord?

Conversely, how many of us grow to bear fruit, giving love, hope and the words of Christ to others?

✝

# Chapter 4

## Seasons

**"Let us fear the Lord our God, who gives autumn and spring rains in season…" (Jeremiah 5:24)**

**"He determines the number of the stars and calls them each by name." (Psalms 147:4)**

**"He covers the sky with clouds; he supplies the earth with rain…" (Psalms 147:8).**

## Springtime Miracles

One time of year I find truly fascinating and exciting is spring. Many folks who live where winters reach extremely cold temperatures find springtime a joyous occasion. Typically from late December through the following March, the daily temperatures are easily below the freezing mark. So, for well over two months and up to about three months in duration, we literally live in an icebox.

From the window of a car, as a motorist passes through on the interstate, it would appear that this place is lifeless and empty. After over two months of ice-cold temperatures, it certainly feels lifeless. Trees, shrubs, grass and other plants stand naked and bare. Colors are limited to black, brown, tan, gray, and all of the drab shades in between. Pretty lonesome colors by many standards. Occasionally, when we get a snowfall, God brightens up our world with some white. It usually doesn't take long after a snowfall, however, for blowing winds to cover the white snow with dust and dirt. It seems as if the freezing, lonely, lifeless period of time called winter will never end.

But then something amazing happens. Temperatures start to rise, days begin to last longer and out of the thawing earth, flowers shoot up everywhere. Daffodils, crocus, tulips, hyacinths… In myriad colors, God once again reminds us of the promise of new life. Even though we think all life is dead and cold, God brings that life back each spring in the form of beautiful flowers. What an inspirational and spiritual time of year. It is a time God gives each of us to renew our faith in Him and come to believe in the promise of everlasting life.

Springtime in my mind is also one of the most splendid opportunities to witness dramatic changes around us. With each spring rain and each warm day, our landscape changes literally right before our eyes. It is such a beautiful time, and it is a time of remarkable contrasts. Very few times throughout the year can you witness the breathtaking color of redbud trees in bloom, with their deep pink and almost purple flowers against the background of light green, as many other trees are just beginning to leaf out. Now add to this splash of pink the bright royal red color of a male cardinal. How about the brilliant plumage of a male blue jay set against a background of deep green pine needles? It is a masterpiece only our Heavenly Father could create so perfectly.

In addition to a fabulous array of colors and the explosion of new life, springtime also hides many treasures for people to find. Morel mushrooms come to mind, tasty little morsels that can be challenging to find. I think that most people have this little book in the back of their mind, filled with pages upon pages of secret maps…

(Page 37. Uncle John's farm, in the woods where I go squirrel hunting. Near the south end there is a deep, wide draw. Along the south-facing slope, there is a fenceline with several dead elm trees above the point where the fence intersects the creek. Good spot. Found 50 or so here last year and the year before.). (Page 51. Reservoir. Take the boat east from the Sandy Point ramp. At the point where the channel narrows, pull up to the north bank at the creek inlet. From the west side of the creek, head northwest about one hundred yards. One large dead tree had over two hundred mushrooms last year.)…

Can you imagine the "fortunes" one could leave their children or grandchildren if they actually took the time to write these mental maps on paper? I think most mushroom hunters get their enjoyment not only from the search and the discovery, but also from the "secret spot" they have found. Perhaps anything written would diminish that pleasure.

People take time off of work and time out of their ordinary day to tromp through the muddy woods, staring at the ground for hours, in search of a few morel mushrooms. Whether it is because of their elusive nature, their taste, or the popularity of it all, mushroom hunting is both challenging and satisfying. Personally, whether searching for mushrooms or making time to meander aimlessly through the forest, with mayapples and trout lilies underfoot and towering oak trees above, I find a sense of God's peace here, and this fills my heart with joy.

Oftentimes, my sense of sight is overtaken by sounds that I hear. The most beautiful of avian sounds to me is the melodious song of a wood thrush on a calm, quiet spring morning.

I know spring has arrived when red-winged blackbirds, yellow-headed blackbirds, bobolinks and meadowlarks return and stake out territory in the pothole country of north central Iowa. Springtime beauty abounds in pine groves, trees which stay green even through the coldest of winters. As spring temperatures warm the soil, I fondly remember masses of bluebells blooming underneath groves of conifers back home on the farm.

The running of maple syrup in the spring is a magnificent example of God's revealing mysteries, as is watching the busy activity of honeybees while trees and flowers blossom. Sit by any river in the spring as the ice goes out and watch the splendid display as large blocks of ice break apart and move slowly downstream. Springtime holds many treasures and changes that refresh my soul.

# Summer

I have fond memories of falling asleep on a warm summer's night to the sounds of a light rainfall. Cool breezes through the open window pushed the curtains effortlessly this way and that, as I drifted off in peaceful sleep. Equally memorable were mornings I was awakened to the gentle, rhythmic sounds of light rainfall. Its soothing and calming sound reminds me of God's reassuring presence.

I vividly recall one late summer night in northeast Iowa, travelling back to my parent's home from a movie with my girlfriend (who is now my wonderful wife). Being about midnight, the world was completely dark, with the exception of millions of stars shining down from the heavens. As I drove northward on that long stretch of blacktop in my dad's car, I noticed some strange lights ahead of me in the night sky. They were so magnificent and awesome, I had to stop the car. Whites, blues, reds, greens, purples, and yellows...all of the colors one could imagine were literally dancing across the northern sky just above the horizon. What an awe-inspiring sight to witness. My eyes moved from the windshield down to the car's dashboard, where a crucifix sat magnetically affixed. As my eyes returned to the dancing northern lights, I gave thanks to God for such awesome natural beauty and splendor.

The spectacular beauty I found in the display of northern lights is one part of summer that gives my soul peace. That being said, however, summers are not always peaceful in nature. Sometimes God sends conflicting masses of air crashing into each other, creating devastating tornadoes. There is no time quite like tornado season in the Midwest. I always feel like there is this ominous, forsaking "edge" to the air. It just seems to hang in the air like a thick, soupy, transparent fog. Livestock mills around nervously, pets behave differently, and even insects subside from their annoying habits. I notice wall clouds forming, usually in the southwest. Winds pick up to hefty velocities, sometimes matching or even exceeding the speed limit on our state highways. Swirling clouds overhead begin to release torrential rain, oftentimes including marble-sized hail. Then, after a short time, it will stop abruptly. It is at this time, during the eye of the storm when God reveals to me His truly awesome, yet mysterious ways.

During the eye of the storm, that ominous edge to the air can once again be felt as the rain subsides momentarily. As humidity wells up from the warm, soaking soil, I notice the color of the sky. Usually gray or dark-toned in run-of-the-mill rainstorms, the skies during tornado conditions are now transformed eerily into yellows and greens. They make me imagine that there is something alien in the air. All at once, the winds revive and sheets of rain pound the earth. It is at this time that you definitely want to be in the basement. During times like these, my mother always lit a blessed candle and we prayed for safety from the storm. God always watched over our home and protected us.

Although severe weather threatens the Midwest each summer, this season is also one full of outdoor recreation and adventure. Fishing for channel catfish and smallmouth bass, calling barred owls, and catching turtles are a few such memorable adventures that come to mind.

Summertime is always a great time to pitch a tent in the backyard or at a park, build a campfire and roast hot dogs and marshmallows. The hot weather is also a perfect reason to go swimming down in the river. Here one can find that special spot along the river's bends that offers a deep pool, filled with cool water. With the sunshine blocked by an overhanging branch from a walnut tree, you can sit and enjoy a rare coolness seldom found in the blazing heat of August.

Nature's beauty abounds in summer. Particularly spectacular to me are fields of goldenrod, coneflowers and black-eyed susans, waving gently in the breeze. Striking, vibrant blooms proudly stand out against a green background of prairie grasses. The Lord brings forth beauty in wild bergamot and blazing star, bottle gentian and culver's root. Myriad flowers blanket our roadsides, despite summer's hottest days.

Before we realize it, the scorching, humid days of summer turn into warm, pleasant ones. God grants us relief once again from the powerful sun. God sends us into yet another exciting season, one of spectacular beauty and change, a season filled with countless signs of the Lord's glorious presence.

# Autumn

Beauty is in the eye of the beholder they say. That being said, I rank autumn as the most beautiful season of the year. When I see a fabulous array of striking colors reflect off the mirror surface of a calm, October lake, I can't help but give praise to the Creator of it all. Autumn is a time when magnificent whitetail bucks nobly cross frost-covered fields with swollen necks and proud antlers. It is a time when muskrats sit lazily atop cattail huts, basking in the sunshine on a brisk November morning. Seeing squirrels rummage among fallen acorns and hickory nuts partly defines autumn in my mind.

During no other season am I able to experience seeing my breath as I partake in an early November pheasant hunt through mature fields of corn. At no other time can I wander timbered trails with leaves at my feet and hundreds more falling from picturesque canopies above. The explosion of a ruffed grouse from its dense hideout makes my heart beat double time. Wild turkeys take to flight from their lofty roosts high upon the bluffs above the Little

Turkey river. Cedars and oaks come to life as I watch these turkeys lumber into flight, one after another, until dozens have become airborne. The sounds they make are quite unique, as I am able to hear branches break by the way of powerful wings.

The fall season holds so many awesome spiritual moments for me that I have only begun to describe a few of them. Making time for reflection outdoors in autumn is especially meaningful for me. Everywhere I look, God seems to be there, showing His beauty in one way, shape or form.

"Lift your eyes and look to the heavens: Who created all these? He who brings out the starry host one by one, and calls them each by name. Because of his great power and mighty strength, not one of them is missing." (Isaiah 40:26) Whether it is the stars of the heavens on a crisp October evening or the splendor of a gray fox sneaking through the forest in the early morning light, I give praise to God for the countless glories given to us in the autumn season.

# Winter

Have you ever awakened on an early winter's morning long before the sunrise to be greeted by an almost fluorescent glow from a full moon? This has happened to me several times, and each time I look out the window at the wintry scene, I am amazed at the wonder and solitude of it all. Still, peaceful shadows of pine and maple weave an interesting web over a smooth blanket of snow. All things behave as if time has stopped, with the moon as a sole source of glowing light. Standing inside a warm home, looking out into the frozen tranquility, I take the time to whisper a prayer. "Thanks God," or "I know You are here with me Lord." Even if the prayer is only a couple of words, it reflects a thankful heart.

Christmas snowfalls, both peaceful and nostalgic, warm the heart and soul. In my mind, celebrating the birth of our Savior is portrayed quite completely with the presence of snow on the ground. It is an association I have had as long as I can remember, one that ties Christmas together with snow. When I look out the window on a crisp, clear

Christmas night, I can see countless stars above snow-covered fields. I try to imagine a star so close that one could follow it. In my mind, I see shepherds and wise men traversing a rocky landscape far away to give homage to a baby, the Savior of the world.

Only a few weeks later in January, we encounter a spectacular phenomenon in the Midwest. It is the mid-winter thaw, and usually lasts about two weeks. Temperatures which typically hover around the bottom of the thermometer, venture up to about 50 or 60 degrees. Hibernating animals, especially striped skunks, awaken for a short spell. And then, seemingly as soon as it arrives, the January thaw disappears into the freezing drifts of snow and ice.

Wintertime miracles are once again revealed as countless branches reach up for the sky like God's children reaching out for Him. Icicles hang from every roof and lake ice continues to build. Whitetail deer and rabbits are much easier to see, as most trees and shrubs have lost their leaves. It is at this time when God challenges us with bitterly cold temperatures and raw, icy winds. God tests our faith and our endurance by allowing us to experience a harsh, freezing climate for two months. After this challenge the Lord sets before us, we are given a marvelous glimpse of the miracle of life, the gift of spring.

"He makes clouds rise from the ends of the earth; he sends lightning with the rain and brings out the wind from his storehouses." (Psalms 135:7)

†

# Chapter 5

## Stories

**"Each one should use whatever gift he has received to serve others, faithfully administering God's grace in its various forms." (1Peter 4:10)**

## Hidden Stones

Have you ever walked through the woods, along the river, or in the fields, looked down, and noticed a jagged, diamond-shaped arrowhead? How about a geode, split in half and beautifully crystallized in its hollow core? Or what about a Lake Superior agate, with its intricate and decorative banding? Opportunities such as these are rare, and the stories these stones tell are ageless and powerful.

Lying in the heart of the Midwest, cycles pass over Iowa, cycles as ancient as time itself. The four seasons come and go each year, and each season brings change. Spring rains erode a little bit more away from the bluffs in

Shimek state forest in southeast Iowa. Winter freezes split up more sandstone at Ledges in Boone County. Summer humidity calls cornfields to flourish near the Loess Hills in western Iowa. Autumn frosts force the bobcat to seek out a winter den in Northeast Iowa's limestone outcroppings.

Somewhere at this moment there is an arrowhead imbedded not so deep in the crevice of a limestone bluff along the Cedar River in Chickasaw County. It is hiding, yet eager to tell its story to some passerby. There is a story of a young native American stalking a magnificent bull elk one drizzly overcast October morning over a thousand years ago. After a painfully long two-hour stalk, the young native finally had an opening to draw his sinew-backed bow and release an arrow. The first two arrows were perfect hits, passing through the lungs and heart. He released a third arrow at fifty yards in an attempt to stop the massive animal before it reached the shallows and crossed the river. The cedar arrow struck a small twig just before it would have passed through the elk's brisket, and it sailed harmlessly over the animal's back and into the limestone bluff across the river. The arrowhead has remained hidden for centuries, it's cedar shaft and turkey feather fletching having long since deteriorated. Each winter, the limestone crevice splits farther apart, and perhaps in twenty more years, it will split far enough for the obsidian point to fall and wash out to the river's edge.

In a field near Fayette, along the Upper Iowa River, a farmer is plowing last year's soybean field in preparation for the new growing season. It is a beautiful spring day, and several large whitetail bucks, which have just recently begun to show this season's antlers, watch the farmer go about his business. As the plow passes over a gradual rise in the center of the field, a glint of sunlight reflects off an agate, deposited in this region centuries ago when Iowa was under massive sheets of ice. This one waits to tell the story of a young native, who used this stone and many like it to play games with other tribal children. This particular boy had been following his father in the tallgrass prairie, making their way back to the village. He noticed a cottontail rabbit out of the corner of his eye, and instinctively reached for the stone. Although his arms were very strong, the potentially lethal stone missed the rabbit's head, and disappeared into the grassy mazes beyond. This agate would not be seen again by the youth, despite several hours of searching.

Hundreds of years and rainstorms later, the stone has moved only twenty yards from where the early native lost it.

The Lake Superior agate will remain there throughout the growing season, as corn rows shoot up on either side of it. Red fox and ring-necked pheasants will pass over it in the early fall, and a hunter will nearly step on it while passing through the field to reach his deer stand. The icy winds will come down out of the north, freezing the agate into the sandy topsoil, until the thaws of March and April next year. It will then be plowed into the blackness for another four years. Myriad treasures such as these are uncovered every year for the individual who is out there looking.

The arrowhead and the agate in these stories remind me of God's enduring patience. A thousand years is but a fraction of a second in God's time. Our Lord's arms are always wide open, waiting for us to return to Him. If only we could simply open our eyes and see. God's unending love surrounds us and has always been there, right in front of us, steadfast and patient since the dawn of time.

# Points of Light

Have you ever been in a truly dark place? Somewhere so dark that you could not even see your hand if you brought it up in front of your eyes? I once heard of a cave tour being led in the Carlsbad Caverns by a federal park ranger. The ranger, using lanterns and headlamps, led a group of hikers into one of the caverns, through numerous narrow passages and deep within the stone walls. When they reached an inner cavern far from the outside world, he had them sit down. Lights were then extinguished. The world went completely black, and they were blind to everybody and everything around them, including their own hands, only fractions of an inch in front of their eyes. As all the participants were beginning to feel quite helpless, the park ranger lit a single match. I can only imagine the power of that single point of light, as it illuminated those people around it and sent streaks of light dancing upward on the cavern walls. I have to believe that this experience would have been awesome to be a part of.

Each of us is a match to our heavenly Father. We are all points of light shining out in a world with much darkness. I want to burn as brightly for my Lord as possible, for I know God smiles at our light, at the times we shine brightly for the sake of His name. For each of us, the day will come when our match will be extinguished. When that day comes, I pray that the Lord will remember those faithful servants, whose lights were beacons of hope to others without.

My sister Debbie has always been an outdoorswoman. I remember a time growing up when she would ask for my help doing different outdoor projects. We called great horned owls (actually *she* did the calling, as my calls sounded like a sick turkey), we gathered and inspected the bones in owl pellets, we looked for morel mushrooms and went fishing and hiking, among numerous other adventures. One adventure I vividly recall was her lantern and bed sheet project. She set up a white bed sheet draped over the clothesline in the backyard, and after dark, we turned on a lantern and set it on a stool between the two halves of the bed sheet. In this way, all of the light was focused onto the white sheets, making them glow brightly in the dark night.

It didn't take long for us to attract quite a collection of moths, beetles, and other flying insects.

It really impressed me how strongly attracted these creatures were to a bright light. This event with my sister is one I fondly remember and particularly think of in a spiritual context. Isn't it true how we as Christians flock to those beacons of light in our lives: pastors, priests, parents, role models, even Christian radio, television and music? Imagine the effect if each of us allowed our light to be seen by the world, if we put it out there for all to see, rather than hiding it deep within ourselves. I can envision the dazzling brilliance God would see, looking down from that glorious heavenly throne.

"You are the light of the world. A city on a hill cannot be hidden. Neither do people light a lamp and put it under a bowl. Instead they put it on its stand, and it gives light to everyone in the house." (Matthew 5:14-15).

# Slower Pace

There was a time I can recall, in the recent past, when I was enjoying the sunshine of a beautiful morning in mid-April. The rotary mower hummed behind me, spinning and cutting with every foot the tractor moved. I was cutting out all of the woody vegetation in a ten-acre prairie we had burned not two weeks past. Although quite dusty, it was an absolutely beautiful morning to be enjoying the outdoors. I started the long task on the eastern side of the prairie, working my way lengthwise down the field, then back. As each pass was completed, it quickly satisfied me how nice the prairie looked without all of the raspberries, locust trees, and dogwoods that had been scattered throughout. On one particular pass, I was mowing near the center of the prairie, and at this location, there was a narrow band of grass, which had survived the fire. As I passed over it, a field mouse scurried out of the tractor's path. "One of the survivors," I thought. As I reached the end of the pass, I turned the tractor around for a return trip. Out of the corner of my eye, I caught a glimpse of movement. Turning my full attention to the scene at hand, I witnessed a red-tailed hawk swoop down into that small patch of grass near where I had just mowed and ascend with a field mouse in its grasp. The survivor didn't make it through this day.

As I mowed, I watched dozens of vehicles pass on the nearby road, most of them travelling at 55 mph, some of them slowing down to see what I was doing. I felt so fortunate at that moment to be travelling at a much slower pace and to be doing what I was doing. Being able to work outdoors has been such a tremendous blessing in my life.

There have been many small daily events such as this in my life that awaken me to the presence of God. With each occurrence, I am renewed in faith and in God's purpose for me. Aren't renewals such as this necessary? Doesn't life get hectic and full? Sometimes it seems as if the schedule book fills up with appointments, events and meetings all too fast. The world seems to demand more and more of your time with each year that passes. I have found that working in the natural world offers me the Lord's peace. Sure, I have appointments, meetings and obligations like everybody else, but spending time in nature each day allows me to take a step back and realize the importance of time in

God's realm. I have found God's peace in a slower pace, and have begun to understand the virtue of patience my parents so earnestly tried to instill in their children.

Small daily events like the experience I described in this story can shape and change each of our lives. Every one of us has stories of our own to tell, tales I believe, which can only be explained by God's residence in our hearts and our lives.

"'For I know the plans I have for you,' declares the Lord, 'plans to prosper you and not to harm you, plans to give you hope and a future. Then you will call upon me and come and pray to me, and I will listen to you. You will seek me and find me when you seek me with all your heart. I will be found by you,' declares the Lord..." (Jeremiah 29:11-14).

&#8224;

# Chapter 6

# Mountains

**"You will go out in joy and be led forth in peace; the mountains and hills will burst into song before you, and all the trees of the field will clap their hands." (Isaiah 55:12)**

That trip was one of the best I can ever remember. My wife and I took a vacation in California with some of my family members. As we began our journey northward out of Los Angeles, it amazed me how the foothills of the San Fernando Valley changed into bunchgrass, tumbleweed and Joshua trees of the Mojave Desert. We continued even further north, and the hills bordering the desert grew larger. More green vegetation was visible, including trees up the mountainsides, indicating the presence of more water. Several hundred miles north of our starting point, we entered into Inyo National Forest, and coniferous trees began to predominate. The mountain peaks of the high Sierras, partially filled with snow, were now all around us.

Countless dense stands of pines and firs surrounded us, like a massive blanket of trees reaching for the heavens. Ageless mountains of rock towered into the heavens and stood among the clouds. There were fantastic formations of rock that inspired awe and demanded respect, formations unmatched by anything human hands could create. I marveled at the seemingly endless miles upon miles of mountains, forests, lakes and streams. Pure, crystal clear lakes sparkled blue in the sunshine, set in front of a background filled with deep forest green.

Through our journey, we visited many beautiful areas in the high Sierras, Yosemite National Park being one of my all-time favorites. On this particular day, I saw first-hand some of the Lord's finest craftsmanship. Enormous towering mountains of solid rock, carved so perfectly, stood grand and proud above me. It is awesome to imagine the power in huge glaciers of ice and rivers of water so many years ago, cutting out these mountains and carving the rock to the shape and form we see it today. Thousand-foot waterfalls cascaded down from high rocky cliffs, shimmering in the sun and sending clouds of mist this way and that in the breeze. Sunlight filtered through countless pine and fir trees, draping soft shadows in such a way that the entire scene resembled a professional painting.

The enormity of some of the trees and boulders truly impressed me. Groves of giant sequoia trees were nestled in the valley floor, with some individuals reaching over three thousand years old. Boulders dot the mountainsides, having broken off years ago from some point above. I witnessed several that were bigger than the house I live in. High mountain meadows, filled with lush grasses and wildflowers flooded my soul with a sense of the Lord's peace.

Amid all of the natural beauty, however, there is evidence of turmoil. Fires, having long since raged through an area, leave miles of dead and blackened reminders of their fury. Avalanches and rockslides tear out virtually every living plant in their path, including enormous conifers, which have weathered harsh winters for hundreds of years. Their path is clearly visible, as vast swaths of forest and vegetation are simply missing all the way down the mountainside.

The mountains hold so many facets of God's work. To me, seeing layers of rocks painted into the broken hillsides is a fantastic treat. Drinking one's fill of life-giving water from a crystal clear mountain stream is an experience that begs me to give thanks to God for such purity. Even the simple patch of wildflowers growing out of a crack in solid rock, or a lone bristlecone pine, which found life high and alone on a steep mountainside, inspires wonder. How awesome it would be to live among such peaceful, steady giants, and to hike their rugged slopes and traverse rocky crags at will.

The Alps in southern Germany, the peaks of the Sierra Madre del Sur mountain range in Guatemala, and volcanic giants in Honduras and Panama are all mountains that I have visited. All of them inspire awe and respect. Each of them reminds me to thank God for such perfect and awesome creations.

†

# Part II

# Faith

**"Now faith is being sure of what we hope for and certain of what we do not see." (Hebrews 11:1)**

Through my daily work duties, I am afforded the opportunity to be surrounded by many of God's finest natural creations. The magnificent scenery I am able to witness each day and season of the year is breathtaking to me. Unfortunately, not everyone has these opportunities. So where can one go to reflect? Somewhere quiet, someplace to think through the troubles and concerns of the day, a place of peace and rest for a weary heart. Although I find nature to be my daily sanctuary for reflection, your space does not have to be in an outdoor setting. I truly believe that if the heart is willing, there are places of solace much closer than we may think. Often times for me, that place may be as close as closing my eyes and taking a seat beneath that old apple tree in Tillie's Woods…

I have found that reflection is something I can do anywhere. I prefer it to be in the forest, along the lakeshore, in the garden or even out in the woodshop while putting a project together. But more often than not, it is while driving in the vehicle, during a quiet lunch at home, while on the lawn mower, in the shower or during numerous daily routines.

God has given us so much to reflect on in our lives. We need to make time to take the focus from ourselves and the stresses of life, and spend time talking with Jesus.

This is the point where I change gears a bit. What follows are the timbered trails where God has found my heart wandering over the past year.

# ✝

# Chapter 7

# Twenty Seconds

**"Set your mind on things above, not on earthly things."**
**(Colossians 3:2)**

I've heard of it happening on television or in books, but only once in a lifetime. Most people probably never have experienced it, yet it happened to me. I can't say it was exactly a calling, but more like an awakening.

It was about 6:30 one Tuesday evening. Supper was finished, dishes were done, and I was at the kitchen table with my two sons. Tyler and Kyle (ages five and two at the time) were drawing pictures on scrap paper and talking non-stop to each other about very important things (talking mostly in a foreign language to the adults in the house, but discussing critical stuff to their developing minds). My wife, Karla was at the computer checking for new e-mail messages, and I sat at the table sifting through one of several dozen woodworking catalogs that found its way into my mailbox. (On more than one occasion I have daydreamed about how great it would be to have all of those tools, however, like a majority of catalogs it would be recycled). The boys continuous chattering carried on as Michael W. Smith sang in the background. It was the only Christian music I owned at the time, but I loved how uplifting it was. All of the sudden, it happened.

My head cleared completely; there were no thoughts whatsoever. At this moment there was no confusion, no disorientation, no imbalance. I knew exactly, *precisely*, where I was. Suddenly an overwhelming, surrounding feeling of God's presence came over me. I felt like I had been awakened for the very first time. My heart clearly focused on one thing: *God.* A sense of enormous peace fell on my shoulders, and then, suddenly the heaviness of life was gone. The very first thought *instantly* entering my mind was, "Take me to heaven with You dear Jesus." I looked over at Karla, who was still busy reading a note on the computer screen. Then my gaze shifted to each of my boys. I could tell they were still talking, but I couldn't recognize what they were saying. My eyes began to well up with tears and again the thought shot through my head.

"Take me to heaven with You." And only moments later, I felt what I believed to be the Holy Spirit move out and I could feel God's grace slip in. The tears did not quite fall and my family did not notice my face, or I certainly would have had a tough time explaining it.

I felt true joy, having experienced some semblance of what heaven truly meant. After these twenty seconds passed, I could not tell you what heaven looked like. I don't know if there were pearly gates or saints and angels everywhere. All I knew, is that whatever heaven had to offer, I wanted it. I *needed* it. I needed it so bad that I needed to leave my family behind without hesitation, without even good-byes. I have never needed anything so badly. Kids may think they need certain toys for their birthday and adults may think they need a sportier car, satellite television, or perhaps a bigger house. But let me tell you, all of the needs or wants I have had *all of my life* could not add up to how much I needed heaven in those twenty seconds. The overwhelming peace I felt is indescribable.

I have an amazing, loving family who means everything to me. We are all in great health, and have been granted many wonderful blessings by God. We come from loving families, have fantastic relatives and friends, we live in a nice home, and we have food on the table every day and a roof over our heads every night. We have rewarding careers that we enjoy, live in a great location, and are surrounded by a great community. We are members of an awesome church family and we listen to God's great servants teach us about Him. And I needed to turn my back on it all, *instantly*, to follow Christ in heaven. There were no bells and whistles, no bright, blinding lights and there were no booming heavenly voices. But, there was twenty seconds of intense mental and spiritual clarity. There was an instant, all-consuming desire to worship at the foot of God's heavenly throne forever. Talk about an eye-opener! This was one for my record books. This one changed my life.

I've heard people say that there are places of heaven on earth. I have not traveled to many resort and vacation spots. But I have to admit that despite the few places in this country and abroad that I have been to, I have not found a place resembling in any way the heaven I came to experience at my kitchen table on that December evening. Some day I would like to take my wife on a cruise, some place where there are white sand beaches and clear, blue shimmering waters. I would like to go to a place where we can relax. A place where we can get away from all the pressures of today's hectic life, even if only for a short time. But even in the most splendid place of tropical paradise, I sense that I will not find the resounding and overwhelming peace I found with God in my twenty seconds. I don't think it will even come close (but seeing as there is only one way to find out, I had best take the cruise and see for myself!).

This kitchen table experience troubled me for a long time. I felt guilty and selfish for desiring God over my own family. I told Karla about this incident and it troubled her too for a long time. But I have come to realize how extremely important it is for us to need heaven. I have come to realize that in an instant we will be parted from all of the earthly ways we know, and we will either be lifted up or cast down. Heaven is no longer some dream place I want to go after I die. It is a place Christ has promised that I will go, and I need to make sure I'm doing everything I can here on earth to get there when the Lord calls my name.

In a way it's strange how twenty seconds can make you take a serious look at your life and search for what is important. Yet, that is just what I have done, and it has made a world of difference to me. Through the passing of each day, there are times when I have difficulty keeping my mind focused on God and following the ways of Jesus. At these times, I take a moment to pray, and I remind myself how much I need heaven:

Dear Lord,

Help me to achieve a perfect heart and soul for the day I meet You. Amen.

It soon becomes crystal clear that I can't afford to stray from the Lord. Use this as your reminder. Although life on earth may be hard, giving in to temptation is not worth losing the chance to spend eternal life with God in paradise. Again, Colossians 3:2 says, "Set your mind on things above, not on earthly things." Follow God.

✝

# Chapter 8

# Faith

**"'...and the one who trusts in him will never be put to shame.'" (Romans 9:33)**

**"He alone is my rock and my salvation; he is my fortress. I will never be shaken." (Psalm 62:2)**

Faith is an amazing thing. I have heard of this kind of incident happening over and over again. I read about it in books and hear about it on the radio and in worship. There is a woman out there who is at the rope's end. It seems that the world is out to get her, nothing more could possibly go wrong, and she tells herself that things could never be worse. She looks up to heaven, not sure exactly why she is doing so, and cries out, "God, please help me." She doesn't know why she is crying out, because she has never truly believed in God. But she cries out, nevertheless, in a last-effort hope that maybe there is a God who is listening.

God shows her the door to a love and salvation so rich, a door that has been standing wide open next to this individual all of her life, but has been pushed aside. Even after a lifetime of sin and materialistic ideals, years of faithlessness and indifference, God does something this woman would never have considered doing. God forgives all the wrongs she has ever committed and welcomes her with open and loving arms into His company.

Dr. Scott Meador, lead pastor at Solon United Methodist Church, on several occasions has called this kind of action by God, "undeserved forgiveness." That was his definition of grace.

The story continues that this woman has since come to know and worship the Lord regularly. She has joined a church family and serves on several committees. She joyfully gives her heart, her time and her money to the Lord, and has found a life far better than she could ever have imagined.

Faith changes people. What started out as a plea for help from a faithless soul unfolded all of the majesty and grace of God's love.  Once God sent down that saving grace, her faith started growing.  Her faith hardly even started out as infinitesimal.  There was almost no faith there.  Yet God knew she would be one of His advocates.  The heavenly Father already had a purpose for her life.  And now her faith is a raging river, speaking out to all that would hear.

Faith is powerful.  It unleashes all of the power of God's grace.  It helps build relationships, congregations, and communities.  Faith has healing power.  Faith builds confidence.  Faith inspires devotion.  One who is secure in faith leads a fruitful life.

Faith to me is my relationship to the Lord.  Faith to me is the complete, unquestioning belief that Jesus Christ died an excruciating death on a cross to save the world from sin.  Faith to me is knowledge that when God calls my name, I'll be going to heaven, all because I put my life, and therefore, my trust in the hands of our Lord.  Faith is my covenant to Him, a promise to honor and worship God and to spread God's message to as many people as I can while I live on this earth.  Faith is a bridge that connects my heart and soul with that of my heavenly Father.  The river flowing underneath is my life.

There is no doubt with a deep-rooted faith. The Lord has already promised eternal life to all who believe in Him and glorify God's name. In life and relationships, sometimes people *act* a certain way in expectation that the end result will be a favorable gain of some kind. Faith is not that way. There is no acting with God. In a faith-filled life, you seek to live like Christ did. Loving your neighbor as yourself is not just something you hear about on Sunday and then forget about on Monday. Faith keeps you in the driver's seat, loving the Lord and excited to share the good news with people you meet. Faith guides you daily to serve the Lord foremost by serving others.

In our daily lives, faith needs to be our big brother. Faith needs to be constantly looking over our shoulder and urging us to make the right choices. I feel that this is all the more reason to continually develop and strengthen our individual relationship with God. As our relationship with God is strengthened, so is our faith. And there is so much more we can accomplish in our daily lives when we have a strong foundation in faith.

Imagine it this way: Build your faith into a fortress, one of stone walls and granite pillars: pillars of love, trust, prayer and devotion. Build your fortress of faith on top of the foundation of Jesus Christ and His teachings. Watch your fortress grow daily. Some days, when it seems the hardest thing in the world to be thankful or prayerful, your fortress may only grow a few stone blocks at a time. Or perhaps, if the hardships motivate you to enter into deeper, more meaningful prayer with God, entire walls may be built on those days. Watch your fortress tower towards heaven, as your faith grows. Guess what happens when you start stepping on God's path more often than the times you stray? It is at this time when your pillars are supporting you fully and allowing you to see God's will for you in your life.

When will your mighty fortress of faith stop growing? The answer for each of us will be different. Mine will never stop. At least not until the day the Lord calls my name, and on that day I will step from the highest level of my fortress directly onto the floor of heaven. I think the more important question to ask is, when will your mighty fortress of faith *start* growing?

When troubled times challenge you spiritually, take refuge in that fortress. Confide in God. Know that God is there by your side, protecting you. Develop an open, honest relationship with the Lord. Increasing your faith will open up so many more doors for you into the Christian life.

Oftentimes I get the feeling that people fail to develop that relationship with God because they think it will take up too much of their time, and so prayers are limited to when extra time is available. My first response to this is, "Who's time?" Most of us have discovered that life is a short and precious thing. None of us knows how much time we have, and so we know that we need to spend it wisely. And that is where most people get off track. Life should not be lived for vacations and holidays, Saturday fishing tournaments and Sunday football games, our jobs and ourselves. Life *needs* to be lived for God. While God is giving us the opportunity to serve Him, we should be nurturing our families, teaching our children by example how to serve others and carry on the message of Jesus Christ. We should be living faithful lives, managing the resources God has given us wisely, and dutifully performing the roles given to us.

A faith-building relationship includes not only being at worship every Sunday, but also time devoted each day to God in prayer. In my mind, it should include reading and studying the bible, and should include heart to heart talks about concerns, troubles and feelings. These are things a lot of men don't feel comfortable talking about or admitting that they talk about. Guess what? When you talk to God during individual times (early in the morning, in the car on the way to and from work, out in the workshop, out on the tree stand or in the bass boat, in the shower, during your exercise routine, etc.) nobody but God can hear you.

Seeing our time as a gift from God, I believe that building faith on a daily basis is so very easy to do. Getting up earlier in the morning, though challenging for some, may be one simple way. Set the alarm thirty minutes earlier than normal, and when you hear it in the morning, remind yourself, "Jesus died on a cross for me. I need to make time for Him." The rest is easy. When I look at it this way, getting up at 3:00 in the morning would be a piece of cake (although I can honestly say I have not yet done this). If mornings are just not an option for you, how about evenings? How about going to bed later in the evening?

Some of the best personal times I have found for strengthening faith have been early morning walks, in the vehicle each day, on the deer stand and while fishing.

There are hundreds of opportunities each day at work for simple little prayers quietly whispered when nobody is around.

I have discovered something pretty neat as a result of my early morning prayers. After having spent time each morning to pray, read from the bible and have a heart to heart talk with God, I feel ready to talk to God all day long. Those morning times build me up for the roadblocks that are bound to happen as I go through the day, and they prepare me to take all of my troubles to God first thing as they happen. By keeping God in my thoughts all day long, I feel that I have become a much more positive person.

# Faith Memories

I always remember God in my life. As a child I was raised going to mass every Sunday without fail, praying before and after every meal, saying prayers before bedtime, and learning about God in religion class. I attended Visitation Catholic grade school in Stacyville, Iowa. I recall learning so much from the teachings I received, and can now see how necessary these messages were to my life. Many great teachers taught countless life-long lessons to me. To these folks, I am forever grateful.

After Visitation, I attended public high school in Osage, Iowa. In high school, I attended a Teens Encounter Christ weekend retreat, which was spiritually uplifting and eye opening to a teenager. Upon graduation from high school I entered the U.S. Army Reserves, and was sent to boot camp at Ft. Leonardwood, Missouri. During my training, I attended Sunday service every opportunity I could get. On one occasion, I was given a weekend pass to visit Fellowship Ranch, a Christian outreach to soldiers. This was time well spent, reflecting on how the Lord was guiding me in my life.

Living at home, I continued to attend mass weekly, however, in college my Sunday attendance relaxed somewhat. I made it to masses about twice a month, sometimes more, sometimes less. Over the next seven years, as a husband and father, worship became even more important and meaningful. There was a need for my family to connect with others in the church family. Although I still felt the Lord in my life, it was not until the winter of 2002, almost ten years later, when I truly came to know the Lord at my kitchen table.

It was a feeling like being awakened, like being able to see clearly for the first time. Once this happened I found myself yearning to hear more about the Lord. I found myself looking for more ways to serve and praise Him and become more involved in church. Coming to know Christ as I have detailed is like nothing I have ever experienced before. In only moments, I felt a love and acceptance of such royal purity and in such magnificent quantity, that it completely changed my life.

I have found that truly knowing Jesus has improved my marriage, improved my relationship with my family and strengthened not only my faith but that of my wife and children.

I have begun to see God's purpose for my life, especially as I reflect on all the events of my life thus far, and this is exciting to see. God is at the wheel, I am along for the ride, and I must say it is a wonderful journey.

# Faith of Noah

In our Christian lives, one of our major goals should be to follow the ways of Jesus Christ. As I think about this, I tell myself that Jesus is perfect, and I will never achieve our Lord's perfection. Has there ever been a human being that has reached faithful perfection? I have read about one who certainly deserves the honor, and that is Noah. This man lived 950 years according to the book of Genesis, and in his lifetime, "…Noah found favor in the eyes of the Lord." (Genesis 6:8). In Chapter 7, verse 1, "The Lord then said to Noah, 'Go into the ark, you and your whole family, because I have found you righteous in this generation.'" In the preceding chapter, the text indicates that the whole world was unjust. "Now the earth was corrupt in God's sight and was full of violence." (verse 11). For one man to find favor with God when the entire world was corrupt seems overwhelming. How much faith does it take for a person to be like Noah? In this book of the bible, God creates the human race. Unfortunately, we turned away from the way of the Lord, and after several thousand years, God destroyed all mankind by means of the great flood, and humanity "started over" with Noah and his family.

Can you imagine how much faith it took to be like Noah? To be so honest, trustworthy and holy as to have God rest the future of all mankind on your shoulders? Do you think you have that much faith? Do you think you could *ever* have that much faith? I believe Noah was a true role model. God found favor in him because he had a thankful, appreciative heart. He toiled on earth, working the soil and did not waste his time on fruitless pursuits or objects. He devoted his life to God and family. When those around him proceeded to sin, his heart and mind stood firm in obeying God's laws.

The more I consider this teaching and God's faith in Noah, the more I am truly amazed. God loves us so much that our Lord is willing to put the future of humanity on our shoulders, if only we would believe in Him with all of our hearts and follow the path of righteousness all of our days. We are entrusted with expanding the Lord's kingdom and it is with honored and grateful hearts that we should accept this way of life.

Notice that I said way of life. Loving others, providing for the less fortunate, serving others, spreading the good news of Jesus Christ and worshiping God is a way of life. It is also what God asks from each of us individually.

"By faith Noah, when warned about things not yet seen, in holy fear built an ark to save his family. By his faith he condemned the world and became heir of the righteousness that comes by faith." (Hebrews 11:7)

† 

# Chapter 9

# Peace

**"For God is not a God of disorder, but of peace."
(1Corinthians 14:33)**

There is a lot to be said for peace. Do you live a tranquil life, or have all of the world's pressures stamped out any hope of a peaceful existence for you? My father is a peaceful man. Being faithful to God and family, being kind to neighbors, going out of his way to help others, being slow to anger and quick to praise; he is my hero, and a true example of how I need to live my life. You hear about people like my parents in books and on television shows. Some people believe individuals such as these are fictitious and cannot possibly be real in today's society and fast-paced world. I can guarantee you that they are real and even more so, they are truly genuine. They don't live in a fairy tale world, a place devoid of hardship, crime and temptation. They do, however, put their trust in the Lord, the one true living God, and as a result, they have been blessed. And I truly believe, because of their faithfulness in Christ, all of their children and grandchildren have been blessed as well. God has blessed them richly in family, in love and in friendship, and in my estimation, they have peace in their lives.

Peace is one of God's grace-filled gifts to us. I'm not certain if I can describe it accurately, but peace to me means having a restful, full heart; being secure with your standing in the eyes of the Lord; and trying to extend that feeling to those around you.

If you have never known peace, can you come to know it? Absolutely! I work outdoors a majority of the year in one of Iowa's busiest state parks. I interact with thousands of people each year (including many under no pleasant terms). Even in the winter months when it gets freezing cold outside, I enjoy staying warm out-of-doors by keeping active. On many occasions I come home exhausted physically from the work I do. Some days I come home mentally exhausted from dealing with difficult people, those who would talk to me disrespectfully before admitting that they were in the wrong. And yet other days, I come home emotionally exhausted, having worked very hard all day long, only to have somebody diminish my feeling of accomplishment by criticizing or complaining about the work I completed. One thing carries me through the hardest of days, and that is God's peace. God reminds me that I have so much to be thankful for, and when that glorious peace settles on my shoulders, our Lord lifts those burdens off and restores my spirit.

It is possible for anybody to know God's peace, as long as they have faith in Him, and have put their lives in those loving and gentle hands.

✝

# Chapter 10

# Challenges of Christian Life

**"I am not ashamed of the gospel, because it is the power of God for the salvation of everyone who believes..." (Romans 1:16)**

Some people I know love riding mountain bikes. There are people who enjoy mountain climbing and rock climbing. I've heard that there are even people who enjoy expeditions to some of the earth's most remote and frozen locations. Each of these outdoor experiences (and many more not mentioned) is challenging in its own way. Perhaps it's the exhaustion one feels as they continually force their legs to push the bike pedals over and over, knowing that soon they will make it to the top of that next hill. Maybe it is the awareness of impending death while ascending a sheer vertical cliff or traversing a rocky precipice. Perhaps it is the gamble that one can defy Mother Nature's harshest of climates. Whatever the challenge, there is typically a good outcome once that hurdle has been cleared. Once the bike rider reaches the top of the hill, they can usually count on an exciting ride down the hill while their legs have a chance to rest. The exhilaration of reaching the summit or standing atop a massive wall you have just climbed must be an overwhelming feeling. Even the popularity and prestige you may earn from surviving in a cruel environment and completing an important objective can leave a person feeling invigorated and full of new energy.

So it is with our lives in Christ. God puts obstacles in our lives for His reasons. Some time after we react to these obstacles (it may be immediate or it may take some time) God allows us to feel good about ourselves. What if we don't always feel that "exhilarating ride downhill" after clearing the obstacle? How we have dealt with the obstacle is largely the culprit. How do you respond to the challenges that God presents to you? Let's start with simple things like the morning you got to your car and found you had forgotten the keys in the house, or that evening after a long day at the office when you left supper in the oven too long and it burned. How about the time you went to the grocery store for milk and instead inadvertently picked up five other things that you remembered needing, but forgot the one thing you came for? Pretty minor hurdles, right? But how did you deal with them? Did you become agitated or irate? Did you yell at the kids, whose usually loud voices seemed to compound the problem? Did it seriously affect your mood for the rest of the day or evening?

Let's move on to more inconvenient challenges. Your status at work is one of arriving "on time." Not early by any means, but on time. This day you had a flat tire. To test you, the Lord has thrown in a light rain shower, no cell phone, the wrong set of wrenches and a spare tire that is stuck on the underside of the car by a rusty locking nut. Ouch! Not the best start to anybody's day, but how do you handle it? In the larger picture, even this incident is pretty minor.

Consider challenges that really set you back. Consider hitting a deer with your vehicle, causing a total loss. How about losing your job, especially at an age when starting over seems incomprehensible, or worse yet, losing your home to a fire. What about the most extreme of life's realities; the death of family members, serious bodily injury or health problems? How would you handle these monumental obstacles?

I submit that as you strengthen and build your faith by reacting positively to the smaller hurdles of life, your faith in God's capable hands will better enable you to survive and cope with the larger obstacles in life.

Why does God put these challenges in our lives, especially when many of them are hurtful and painful? I have heard it said that God challenges us so we may realize how imperfect and incomplete we are in this world. Our Lord gives us challenges so we may realize how much we depend on His divine intervention and how much we need God in our lives.

How we deal with roadblocks in our life is our gift to the Lord. God asks us to be spiritually responsible. God is not the source of our problems, but rather, *the solution*. When bad things happen in life, our response is one indication of how well we honor our heavenly Lord.

# Working for the Lord

One bible passage I refer to almost daily can be found in the New Testament in the book of Colossians. Chapter 3 verse 23 reads, "Whatever you do, work at it with all your heart, as working for the Lord, not for men." These are truly words to live by. Another, very similar in word and meaning can be found in 1 Corinthians 10:31, "…whatever you do, do it all for the glory of God."

Whenever I search for a true example of this verse, I think of my mother. She was a housewife, holding the job title of mom, and having broad general knowledge as a cook, janitor, maid, doctor, teacher, therapist, counselor, enforcement officer, singer, preacher, coach, banker, mechanic, handyman, and even exterminator (among *countless* others). So many years she spent devoted and committed to her Lord and family. As long as I can remember she has always cheerfully cooked award-winning meals, and has always been satisfied with short words of thanks like, "Delicious supper, mom." I am certain there have been times when no thanks were given at all. She has patiently served her family and others over her lifetime, expecting nothing in return. Raising eleven children and keeping up with cleaning in a two-story home was a monumental task, but it was one she performed as if serving the Lord. Fervent and faithful in prayer, my mother has been guided by the Lord all of these years and continues daily in her walk with Him. My mother has given and sacrificed more than any other person I've known in my life. She truly follows the examples of Christ, and gives me a clear path to follow.

How often in your job do you feel like your boss or your employer is hard to work for, perhaps even impossible? Conversely, maybe your employer has the best employee benefits, looks out for you, and treats you well. I would imagine most people fall somewhere in between the two. One thing we all need to remember is who brought us to this place in our lives. Who opened the door for you and gave you that job? Who directed and orchestrated your life leading up to that point, allowing you to make choices along the way, but gently guided you toward an unseen will? God, of course. The Almighty Lord put you here for His reasons and a much higher purpose.

In these bible verses from Colossians and first Corinthians, "whatever you do," means simply that. These verses do not mean we get to pick and choose the times or tasks that we want to put our full efforts into. God wants us to do everything as if working for Him. This includes not only medial tasks like cleaning the house or performing our daily jobs, but also how we speak, think and act. Personally, this means putting God at the very center of each thought I process, each word I speak and each action I perform.

Opportunities may arise to take advantage of your employer, be it company time, supplies, computer resources, whatever. It may be very easy to do personal business on company time or cheat an employer out of a few minutes here or there. Always remember that you are working for God. You will be held accountable for your actions on the last day. The Lord gave us clear commandments to follow, and none of them include the words, "most of the time."

God wants us to stay busy and be productive people. God wants us to fulfill our earthly roles to the best of our abilities. So serve your employer faithfully and honestly.

But be a company man or company woman for God. Do all things as if working for the Lord.

# God's Will

Many times we pray to the Lord and request God's help. For some, it is many times a day, for others only occasionally. Whether it be a request for something as important and potentially complicated as starting your life over in a new place, or something simpler such as asking God to guide your day and stay by your side as you begin a challenging work week, keep in mind that the Lord hears every prayer. God will also answer your prayer, but on God's time, not yours. The Lord's answer may not always be what you want to hear, but realize that God's will shall come to pass.

Wherever you work, whatever you do, strive to see yourself in the position you are because of God's calling you to that position.

Focus on the Lord and search your heart. Ask yourself some challenging questions: Why is it God's will for me to be working here? What has God called me to do at this place? How can I better serve the Lord at my job and in my daily life? When these questions can be answered honestly and clearly, you will know the Lord has opened the door to another room in your heart. It is a big room, with plenty of space for lots of friends to come over and visit, a room overflowing with God's love and grace.

# Fearing Death

One of life's greater challenges in my estimation is clearing the hurdle of fearing death. We spend much of our lives seeking enjoyment and self-fulfillment. Knowing that an end to our lives will invariably sneak up on us can be a stressful issue to face.

I no longer fear death. Yes, seeing and hearing the horrific, painful deaths of others across this country and this world makes me shudder. They make me pray silently for those who have suffered, and they make me pray that I never have to endure that pain. Seeing these tragedies reinforces my need to live a slower and more safety-conscious life.

However, I know my days are numbered. That is one guarantee God has given each of us. We will all part from this earth. For quite some time, I have believed that my life is in God's hands. It is not up to me to decide when my life on this earth is over, for that right is God's alone. So as strongly as I have felt the need to gain a heavenly home someday, I know and understand that the Good Lord will choose that time for me. Isaiah 57:1-2 covers this issue well. "The righteous perish, and no one ponders it in his heart; devout men are taken away, and no one understands that the righteous are taken away to be spared from evil. Those who walk uprightly enter into peace: they find rest as they lie in death."

When my final day comes, I will hear God's voice calling my name. And whether I am leaving this world in restful sleep or in the most agonizing pain possible, I'll know in my heart that my true, everlasting journey will soon begin. I envision the Lord's voice to be like that of my dad, with his hand gently shaking my shoulder and saying, "Wake up son. It's time." God's sweet voice will be gentle and soothing, and no other sounds will I hear. I will not be afraid, for I will be going home.

# Test Yourself

We need to challenge ourselves to take God public. Don't keep Him a secret. Does God embarrass you? Are you ashamed to say God's name out loud? Are you fearful of alienation by your friends and family? Some people use the phrase, "walk a mile in my shoes sometime." I submit that most people could not walk ten feet in the sandals of Jesus Christ.

Test yourself: 1) Take your bible to work and read a chapter before you begin, in full view of everyone else. Also, leave the bible on your desk in full view of anybody who should pass by. 2) Listen to a Christian music station at work or when driving in the car with a friend or co-worker. Buy an album of praise and worship music and leave it on your desk at work for anybody to see. 3) At a restaurant, before you begin your meal, say a prayer. If you have a spouse or family, hold hands and say your prayer aloud. Even if you are with a co-worker, say it aloud, or better yet, ask them to join you.

Three simple tests...how would you do? Would you feel comfortable doing any of these three? Would you feel anxious, nervous, worried? If you have trouble with these simple tests of faith, pray. Ask God to give you the courage to be a disciple for Him. Don't hide from God, and don't be ashamed or embarrassed, for the Lord's endless love is a gift in this life that we should all embrace and celebrate.

# Life is Too Short

I have been very blessed. Every day, I see or hear about addictions to drugs, alcohol, gambling, sex, money, and countless other evils all around me in this world. Thanks needs to be given to the watchful care of my heavenly Father for granting me resistance to these deadly snares.

So having never been a prisoner to addictions, I cannot begin to counsel anybody on the best ways to break free from the bonds of these diseases. I cannot offer any 12-step programs. I am no more qualified to treat these afflictions than I am qualified to perform brain surgery. Most assuredly, I cannot begin to understand the vices that must rule the daily life of a person caught in an addiction. And although my faith is probably light years away from that of my parents or my pastor, I do feel qualified to recommend turning one's life over to God as the solution.

I feel qualified to do so because each one of us in this world is a child of God. The Lord is our loving Father, and God has asked each of us to glorify Him by telling others about the way of the cross. Real life is full of hardship, temptation and strife. Allow God to be that rock that you lean on for support, and confide in God for an everlasting supply of strength and encouragement.

"Since you are my rock and my fortress, for the sake of your name lead and guide me. Free me from the trap that is set for me, for you are my refuge. Into your hands I commit my spirit; redeem me, O Lord, the God of truth." (Psalm 31:3-5)

## †

# Chapter 11

# Stewardship

**"Be sure to set aside a tenth of all that your fields produce each year." (Deuteronomy 14:22)**

**"'A tithe of everything from the land, whether grain from the soil or fruit from the trees, belongs to the Lord; it is holy to the Lord...The entire tithe of the herd and flock—every tenth animal that passes under the shepherd's rod—will be holy to the Lord.'" (Leviticus 27:30, 32)**

I struggled with this chapter, as it deals with a private matter between each Christian and the Lord. That matter is stewardship and our gifts to God.

Over the past year, the Holy Spirit moved me to change my family's level of giving. Please know that this is not a chapter about self-righteousness. My family has never and will never be that way. Rather, this note precedes one brief experience with God's Holy Spirit in my life, and how I hope that this particular change in my faith can help expand the Lord's kingdom through the lives of other Christians.

Now, I don't know where you are at with your journey in stewardship. To me, this is a matter of faith that we must each address individually. I believe that God smiles on all generosity toward His holy church. I also believe that God will, at one point or another and in one way or another, speak to each Christian's heart about stewardship.

One of my responsibilities at work is to protect and enhance this state's natural resources. This includes the removal of invasive and exotic species, the establishment of native, desirable species and the maintenance of what resources are already in place. I think God wants us to view our lives in much the same way. In simplest terms, cut out the bad stuff, put in the good stuff and then take care of it. God wants us to be good stewards, not only of the earth where we live, but also of our own lives and of the Lord's holy church. One means of stewardship is tithing, giving back to God the first ten-percent of what we earn.

Well, something changed. It was several weeks after my twenty-second experience at the kitchen table. The day the change came, I was building and painting picnic tables, as part of my normal wintertime duties at work. As icy winds howled outside of the three-stall shop I was working in, I listened to a pastor on the radio talk about our gifts to God. He brought up the subject of tithing and how he had been preaching to his congregation on this topic one Sunday. During his sermon he spoke of God's promise to us that God would provide for us if we gave back to Him the first ten percent of what we had. The pastor then went on to tell about a particular individual who approached him after the worship service had ended. This individual had heard his sermon, but was reluctant to give ten percent because he was barely making ends meet financially as it was. He asked the pastor if in giving ten percent, at the end of the year the pastor would make up for any shortfall he may incur over the course of the year. The pastor then asked the individual, "Are you telling me that you are more willing to put your faith in me, an ordinary man, above your faith in God?" The radio went silent for a few moments as the pastor let it sink in. Did it ever sink in.

It was at this point when I lost all sense of the broadcast and truly heard God's words in this pastor's voice. The overriding feeling of guilt weighed heavily upon my shoulders. So heavily in fact, that on this particular afternoon, I broke down onto my knees and prayed. Something inside my head and heart suddenly made me aware that I had to make the change today. Just like the snapping of one's fingers, I knew it had to be today. God had been asking my family to give Him the first ten-percent of what we earned. Not the leftovers. Not the scraps. Not only when budgets allowed for giving a little extra. God asked us to give to God *before anything else.* It was that day I realized that what little we had been giving was not being faithful to God.

That afternoon was a long one for me. I knew that sacrifices would have to be made, as we were on a tight budget the way it was. And so that night, after a long afternoon of prayer, I talked to Karla about the joy I had found in God. I told her how my faith relationship had developed stronger than I ever imagined. I also described the twenty-second experience I had undergone at the kitchen table, which upset her greatly. After spilling forth feelings and emotions for quite some time, I told her about my need for our family to begin tithing. I made it clear that

I was willing to give up every material thing I had or wanted, in addition to the hobbies and pastimes I enjoyed (hunting, fishing and woodworking to name a few) all so we as a family could give ten percent to God. I continued on, pleading that God wants our gifts to be joyful and heartfelt, and I hadn't truly felt that way yet, giving as a family. Second Corinthians 9:7 reads, "Each man should give what he has decided in his heart to give, not reluctantly or under compulsion, for God loves a cheerful giver." God doesn't want our gifts to be given with grumbling or regret. To make a long and difficult story short, that night we won a victory for God and for our family.

In my family when I was growing up, tithing was first and foremost. That first ten-percent spent was on God. Even though it seemed that money must be tight, God always provided for our family. God always ensured our well being. And although I grew up watching my parents give faithfully to the Lord, I never had a solid grasp of what tithing truly meant. As a student in college, my weekly giving was often times a few dollars and occasionally five or ten dollars. After college, having started a family, our giving was consistently around twenty dollars a week. This went on for six or seven years. Over the last three years, as our means increased, we also increased our giving. Our gifts were heartfelt, but with all of the bills and budgeting items we had to take care of financially, I didn't think we could afford to give ten percent. Little did I recognize that God was in control, not me.

I want to testify to the abundant blessings and peace we have received because of this sacrifice. There have been numerous times where my family was running short, and bills loomed over our heads like dark storm clouds ready to loosen their rain. But God has always come through, sending that unexpected check when it was most urgently needed, getting us through some rough months when larger bills were due and seeing to it that we always had food on the table and a roof over our heads.

All gifts to God are important and necessary, and each Christian must decide individually in their heart what those gifts will be. God gives us what we have out of His generous heart. The Lord pours out blessings in many forms: good health, happiness, peace, joy, food on the table, a place to live, heat in the winter, clothes to wear, good jobs...just to name a few. And so our giving back to the

Lord needs to imitate the abundant generosity our Lord has so openly and freely shown to us.

Understanding that all we have belongs to God, is a crucial first step. God wants us to be thankful and appreciative people. Knowing that you give openly to the Lord *with a joyful heart* is a wonderful feeling.

# Get Rich

I once read an article about a man whose main goal in life was for his last name to be a household name across America. He was one day going to be rich and famous. I do not know where this man is in his faith journey right now, but his statements have made me think a lot about our society as a whole. All around us in this country people are scrambling to make an extra dollar. Social pressures seem to tell us to make more money, have more things, be more comfortable. Well, guess what happens next? God calls your name. Your match is extinguished, and all you can carry with you is your soul. As Timothy 6:7 reads, "For we brought nothing into the world, and we can take nothing out of it." Are you ready to answer the Lord's questions? Did you help the least of My people? Did you provide clothes to those who were naked? Did you give food to those who were hungry? Did you give shelter to those without a home? Did you tell others about Me? And the most important question, now that your life on earth is over: *Where are you going now*?

How much more important it seems to me that we should be making *God's* name a household name across this country and across this world. I want my major goal in this life to be the attainment of heaven, but only after the life our Lord has given me here on earth has been filled to His satisfaction with faithful service to the kingdom. I want to try and make God and His son, Jesus Christ, household names. In my mind, there is nothing wrong with being wealthy, having success and many earthly possessions, as long as what one has helps expand God's kingdom. Open your heart to the possibilities of the Holy Spirit, and give your life to God. Our Lord will give you riches beyond your wildest dreams!

# Comfortable

One July afternoon, I was working along a lakeshore trail trimming back tree branches. It was an awesome day, filled with sunshine and warm weather. Squirrels were scampering across the forest floor and chasing each other from one tree to the next. A red-bellied woodpecker alighted to the side of a dead elm tree nearby and began winding its way around the bare trunk, looking for a meal. As I stopped my activity to take all of it in, my eyes shifted from the forest and out across the calm lake waters. A couple of men were out fishing in their small boat about a hundred yards down the lakeshore. Beyond them, on the opposite shore, is where I noticed the house. Actually, I had seen this house many times before, as I knew that it was just a summer cottage, but this day was the first time I had really noticed it. It was a beautiful lakeshore home with fine landscaping and retaining walls, in addition to its own private dock and pontoon boat. Several century-old sentinel oak trees towered in the yard, with branches reaching out, trying to touch the elegant veranda along this home's second level.

The first thought entering my mind was that whomever owned this summer home must be financially "comfortable". I quickly realized that my wife and I would never be able to afford a home such as this. It was truly a house that most people dream of having.

My thought process continued, recalling how little need we had. God had kept a roof over our heads, food on the table and kept us working at solid full-time jobs all these years. God blessed us with a healthy family, all of our senses, full use of our limbs and faculties. The Lord gave us the ability to walk, run, jump, open doors, cook meals, play piano, build, write, draw, stitch and sew, drive a car, plant a garden, dance to music, take pictures of our children and play fetch with our dog (among countless others).

God gave Karla and I loving, devoted, and faithful parents, bountiful siblings to grow up with and learn from, and now our generous Lord has given us each other and two wonderful children. God has granted us more blessings than I could possibly find paper to write them all down on. Comfortable? No. But rich? Yes friends, we are very rich in the blessings of God. Perhaps if I were pessimistic by nature I would tell myself that this is little comfort when the paychecks run out all too soon. Perhaps I would try to convince myself that being comfortable financially would be a lot better lifestyle than the one we are presently living. But I have felt the presence of God in our lives, and I know that we have much more than we need. Much more than we even deserve. Yes, we are rich in the Lord's blessings.

In my faith journey, I have found one reason in the scriptures, which explains this wealth of blessings. The Old Testament book of Deuteronomy 7:9 says, "Know therefore that the Lord your God is God; he is the faithful God, keeping his covenant of love to a thousand generations of those who love him and keep his commands."

Due to the fervent prayers and faithful service of our parents and possibly many generations before them, God has given us abundant blessings. I want my children to be as very blessed as we have been, and that is yet another reason my heart will praise the Lord's holy name and spread the good news of Jesus Christ. It is one small reason why I will raise my children to know and worship the Living God.

✝

# Chapter 12

# Christian Reality

**"I know, O Lord, that a man's life is not his own; it is not for man to direct his steps." (Jeremiah 10:23)**

**"...'My grace is sufficient for you, for my power is made perfect in weakness.'..." (2 Corinthians 12:9)**

Perhaps at this point you get the impression that I don't have a clue about today's culture and reality as we know it. In many ways, living in small town Iowa, I would have to agree that I am not "in tune" with big city culture. But let me tell you, there is another completely awesome "reality" out there. It is a reality centered on our Lord Jesus Christ, no matter where you live. Once you *truly* come to know Jesus, you will find that what I have written about thus far is not fictitious and is certainly not a result of a warped sense of reality.

Once I came to know Jesus Christ in my heart, the spiritual side of my life became *my whole life.* If I could categorize myself developmentally in my spiritual life, however, I would only consider myself a toddler. I am still learning to communicate God's message as He would have me do. I am still wobbly and unsteady as I try to learn to walk down the Lord's path. Often times I find myself stumbling. Above all, I am still learning many new and exciting ways I can serve and honor the Lord in my daily life.

This Christian reality is not exempt from sin, suffering, temptation and injustice. On the contrary, the Christian reality I have come to know works to drive out sin, ease suffering, avoid temptation and bring justice to a world full of need.

For many years of my life I have been a selfish person, always striving for self-fulfillment and trying to acquire possessions that would supposedly make me happy. Thanks to the Lord in my life, I am beginning to see new ways of conducting business, so to speak. I still have hobbies that I enjoy, such as writing, woodworking, gardening and even beekeeping, but I am finding ways to use those pursuits for God's gain. My daily work life is centered around fulfilling God's will by serving others and protecting our natural resources. My home life is centered around fulfilling God's will by raising our two children to follow biblical principles. My marriage is centered around fulfilling the Lord's will by growing together with my wife in faith and love, by keeping prayer an integral part of our relationship and by our combined service to God.

As Christians, I feel we need to enrich our lives in the Lord. Our Christian lives require more than just going to worship on Sundays. Individually, we need to develop a relationship with Christ. Talk to the Lord each day and make time for Him. Take everything to God in prayer. Not only should we talk to the Lord, we need to open our hearts and listen. Listen to God's will in our lives. Hear what God would have you do in your life. Growing in faith should be something we seek to accomplish each and every day.

As your faith is strengthened and renewed, God's calling in your life will be more evident. There is a true urgency in spreading the words of Jesus Christ and completing Christian work at every possible opportunity.

To hammer out my point, there is another whole world out there taking up the exact same time and space we currently occupy, however, it is one centered around God rather than self. From personal experience, I can testify that there is endless peace, joy and fulfillment for those who come to know Jesus Christ and experience the Christian reality.

# No Excuses

At times, we have all made excuses for not going to worship on Sundays, for not helping out our family or friends, or for not getting involved in congregational functions. Let me be the first to admit that I have made my share of excuses.

Chances are, at some point in time, all of these opportunities you have passed over will finally catch up with you. You will come to a realization making you feel ready to seek reconciliation and ready to get involved. When this realization hit me last year, I remember feeling like I had been trying to "get out of doing the chores" so to speak. I felt like I was skimping God and cheating our Lord out of His purpose for me.

Don't make excuses for neglecting God's work, especially if you know in your heart that you have the time and resources to serve Him. One of the most popular excuses (and I am guilty of this) I am quite certain people use is that of having young children. Children can make running errands, attending functions, and serving others inconvenient and many times difficult. You need to ask yourself, "Am I unable to accomplish this service with the children along, or am I simply electing not to because I don't want to deal with the hassles of loud, energetic children running around everywhere and not listening?" There are many inherent qualities children have which give people good reason not to participate. But think of all the people who could have been helped or the services that could have been performed, had you only decided to brave it and take the children along. I think the world would be a much different and better place if there were no such thing as excuses.

In addition, the children learn about serving God and others at a young age, something that is happening less frequently these days. Even if you think they are too young to understand, explain to them how you are helping others, and *God will allow it to sink in.* Your actions help develop Christian hearts in your children.

If you have children, take a minute to think of them and pray for them now. Wouldn't it be worth the time and effort if your actions guide your children's hearts to be God's servants as they mature?

Although children tend to be one of the major excuses, there are many others. Do you feel uncomfortable participating? If so, then pray. Ask God to help you open your heart to His will. Brainstorm ways that you and your family can be of service. There is always middle ground. There are many ways to serve the Lord that do not require being up in front of the congregation at worship time. Making cookies and bars for fellowship time, visiting the sick, visiting the elderly, delivering donated goods from church to a shelter, giving to Goodwill...are just a few examples in a very long list of ways to serve. Perhaps you are good at painting or cleaning, maybe handy in home repairs, talented at woodworking. The wheels should be turning in your head at this point.

God calls us all to serve. A select few are called as pastors and priests. The majority of us are called to serve in smaller, but no less important capacities. Each of us needs to discover what that calling is. One thing I am completely certain of is that God has a higher purpose for each one of us. We hold the jobs we do and live where we do, not as a result of our efforts, coincidence or luck, but rather by the will of God. We are brought to this place and time to fulfill a purpose for the Lord. When we stop making excuses and begin to serve the Lord with a joyous heart, that calling becomes clear.

"From one man he made every nation of men, that they should inhabit the whole earth; and he determined the times set for them and the exact places where they should live. God did this so that men would seek him and perhaps reach out for him and find him, though he is not far from each one of us. 'For in him we live and move and have our being...'" (Acts 17:26-28)

# The Eye in the Sky

We all knelt huddled together in a circle, with helmets off, panting from exhaustion after a scorching August high school football practice. Coach gave us a minute to catch our breath and get situated before he gave us the "good job today, men" speech. The grass of Sawyer Field, our antagonist during practice, now felt relaxing as we let our heartbeats slow down to a medium roar. Coach grabbed our attention. "Men, look up there." He pointed to the press box above the home stands. "That's what I call the eye in the sky. It does not lie. If you're slacking, if you're missing your assignments, if your shoes are not tied, the eye in the sky will show it. When we watch the tapes on Saturday morning, everybody else will know it, and then guess what? I'll be talking to you!" After the brutal practice we had just endured, we all silently agreed that the eye in the sky was not going to let us be its first victim.

When I think back to the glory years of high school football and the "eye in the sky," I can draw a direct parallel to that of our heavenly Creator. God is our eye in the sky.

Our Lord knows not only what we do and what we say, but also what is on our minds and in our hearts. Nothing gets past God, nothing at all. It may or may not be a Saturday morning, but the day will come when everything we have done, said, thought or felt will come to light. How do you want Coach to speak to you on that day?

# Best Friends

Now, I don't know about you, but I have a best friend in my life. She is my wife. Karla and I have spent 15 years as best friends, sharing countless movies, dinners and conversations together.

I am also blessed to have many very close friends, people who I consider best friends. People I have known since high school and college, who are caring and generous. Some I played football, basketball and ran track with. Others I served with in the military or worked with over the years. Still others were weight lifting partners, actors and sports buffs with me.

Each year at Christmas time or at birthdays, Karla and I exchange gifts, just as most other couples I know. But these material gifts simply cannot compare to the gifts that our Savior has given us. Keeping this in mind, how often do we talk to God compared to our best friends? For all that the Lord has done for us, talking to God should be the absolute highlight of each moment.

If God is truly in our lives and hearts at every moment, He is more devoted to us than our very best of friends. I greatly enjoy the opportunities I am allowed to speak with my best friends. I can only guess that the same holds true for you. So what holds you back from speaking to God? After all, God gave us the gift of life. Our Lord has also forgiven us for our sins by sacrificing Jesus Christ on the cross at Calvary. God offers us the promise of eternal life for following Him and spreading the good news of Jesus Christ.

# The Interstate

One evening, driving southbound alone down the interstate in my family's minivan, I noticed a truck and pop-up camper pulled off of the roadway along the northbound lane. In only moments, I recognized that this individual had some major problems, as the side of the camper closest to the ditch did not have a wheel and was resting on the gravel shoulder. Nobody else had stopped, and the individual was still in his truck. Trying to remember this section of interstate, I fought to remember where the next interchange was where I might turn around.

Immediately I said a quick prayer, "Bless this individual Lord. If you would have me help, please let one of the next three overpasses have an exit where I can turn around."

The next three overpasses had no exit. I had traveled what seemed to be at least five miles. After the third overpass was behind me, I prayed again. "O Lord, I am sorry that I did not turn around to help, but…" At that point I stopped and my heart took over. Listening closely, I could hear God telling me to go back. One mile ahead was an exit, where I turned the van around and headed back. I prayed yet again, "God, I feel You pulling me this way. If it's Your will, allow me to help out somehow."

As I arrived, I saw that another group of four individuals in a truck had stopped. As I walked up to them, I asked if I could be of any help. Sean, the owner of the camper explained that the lug nuts had sheared off and the tire was wedged above the axle in the fender well. These men had already lifted up the camper by hand and put a jack underneath to support it. One of the passersby was on the ground, underneath the camper trying to figure a way to get the tire out. Matt was his name, and he suddenly came up with what seemed to be a great idea. He used a small hydraulic jack to try to press the tire downward, away from the camper's frame. His companion and obvious friend said to him, "Well, you better give credit to Jesus Christ for that one because you know you're not smart enough to come up with that on your own!" A big smile crossed my face…the four men who stopped before me were Christians, and were using this opportunity to spread God's message to a stranger. Right away I noticed that Matt needed some tools to get the hydraulic jack working. The only ones to be found were "coincidentally" the only two tools in my vehicle that came with the spare tire kit. Although at first it seemed to be working, after five minutes, we could tell that his efforts were forcing the tire more into the fender well than downward.

I looked at him and said, "How about if you tried to push the fender well outward by bracing the jack against the leaf spring?" A light bulb turned on in his eyes, like he just saw something he had overlooked. Without a word, he removed the jack, re-situated it against the leaf spring and began pressing the fender well outward. I silently whispered a breath prayer to myself, "Please let this work, Lord." Within a minute, the tire fell from the fenderwell. Remarkably, it was still in operable condition, only missing the lug nuts that had sheared off. Immediately, the vocal one of the Christians looked at the owner and said, "Well, now you *have* to go to church this Sunday!" To make a long story short, everything turned out fine.

I couldn't get the smile off of my face, heading home that night. I gave God thanks for guiding five Christians to help this individual in need. Although it may seem pretty insignificant to some, the event was profound to me. What a joy it was to know that God used me in His perfect way, as only God can. The Lord asked me to stop along the interstate on that particular night to help with that one particular task. Would the other four Christians have figured it out? In my heart I believe that they would have, but it brings peace to my mind and joy to my soul, knowing that God asked me to be there and to be a part of the Christian message.

# Failures

My life has been full of failures. Failure to be honest, failure to make the right choices. Failure to be a faithful servant to our Lord. I recognize the mistakes I have made in my life and have laid them at the feet of Jesus. Because of Christ's ultimate sacrifice of love for me, I know that He has forgiven me, cleansed me of my sins, and even erased those sins from memory. Jesus told the harlot in the gospel of Luke (7:48,50), "...'Your sins are forgiven,'" and "...'Your faith has saved you; go in peace.'" Also, in John 8:11, Jesus stated to the adulteress woman, "...'Then neither do I condemn you,' Jesus declared. 'Go now and leave your life of sin.'" Likewise, Jesus has asked me to stay on course and follow his path of righteousness.

Financial companies tell us, "Past performance does not indicate future results." Likewise, I know my past mistakes cannot dictate my future victories. And that is exactly what the right choices are to me...victories. When opportunities arise for me to sin and I choose not to, I have just won a major battle for the Lord Jesus Christ. And do you know what? I truly believe our Savior smiles with each victory I win.

We are human and we are sinners. We have disobeyed God's rules in our lives. We have not followed the teachings of Christ. Yet, by the ultimate sacrifice that Jesus gave for us on the cross, we know that we are forgiven. We know that even in our human weakness, God's love for us is so great that our transgressions are forgiven and we are given a fresh start, a second chance.

"…set your hope fully on the grace to be given you when Jesus Christ is revealed." (1 Peter 1:13)

# Dead End

One sunny morning, I sat at the end of the lane in our family's vehicle waiting for the school bus to pick up my son Tyler. It was a beautiful late winter morning, and the sun had risen behind me high enough in the sky to spread its abundant light over the frozen lake and timbered shorelines. Michael W. Smith sang "Breathe," one of my favorite songs, on the radio. I turned up the music slightly, closed my eyes and focused on the words. Towards the end of the song, as he repeated one of his lines, he sang out, "I'm lost without You." Immediately after this verse, I opened my eyes. The very first thing my eyes focused on was a yellow diamond-shaped sign across the intersection shining, almost to the point of glowing, with the rising of the sun behind me. It read in bold letters, "Dead End."

I found this to be a pretty significant event. As I sat reflecting on this, I could see how true it is when somebody does not have the Lord in his or her life, it is like driving down a dead end road. There may be a lot of fantastic houses, beautiful scenery, and perhaps even fun places to stop and recreate. But as you get to the end, you realize that you've made some mistakes. Now there is nowhere further that you can go. Your only option is to turn around go back to get on the right road, the road to God. This is the only avenue that will lead you somewhere truly purposeful.

†

# Chapter 13

# Purpose

**"And we know that in all things God works for the good of those who love him, who have been called according to his purpose." (Romans 8:28)**

As I write these words, my belief that God has a purpose for my life is being reinforced. Almost two years ago, an opportunity came up for me to re-enlist in the Army Reserves, to continue serving with a circle of friends that had become a family to me over the past twelve years. At that time, I felt a strong pull away from military service, despite many great benefits I received at work for being a service member. The monthly checks I received for attending Army Reserve drills were not fantastic, but they did help pay the bills. I felt uncomfortable leaving at the twelve-year point, when only eight more years would earn me retirement benefits. Mostly, I was troubled turning my back on that group of friends who had become like family to me, many of whom had the same choice of re-enlistment as I did, and chose to stay.

Yet, through all of the turmoil clouding my decision, one voice rang out with a vibrant echo, "Please come home to your family." It was Karla's voice, sweet and pleading. She had seen me gone too many weekends already. Over the course of twelve years, one would be surprised how many birthdays, anniversaries and special occasions I had missed.

Although I felt the decision had been made well before my last day, it was much harder to actually do than I had ever imagined.

You may be wondering how I feel that this may be for God's greater purpose. To be honest, I didn't recognize it as God's will until it became evident that our country was once again going to war in the Middle East. In February 2003, Bravo Company of the 389th Engineer Battalion, located in Decorah, Iowa was called to active duty to provide humanitarian aid in Operation Enduring Freedom. This was the Army Reserve unit I had been a member of only 20 months prior, the circle of friends I knew as my second family.

When I got the call from Hondo, a retired member of Bravo Company and great friend who I had served under, my heart sunk. Many great friends would now be leaving families, homes, careers and all the freedoms they enjoyed serving our country half a world away.

That phone call told me that God had other plans for me. My wife could have chosen to mislead me and could have encouraged me to continue my military service. But instead, I could not help but notice the pain and loneliness she and the boys felt when we were apart. She was honest with me and encouraged me to stay at home with my family. If she had chosen to mislead me, or if I had elected to sacrifice more time away from my family when that opportunity arose, then I would now be spending over a year of my life away from her and my two sons.

It is easy for me to see now, how God had intervened all of these years. The Lord humbled my heart, making me aware of my family's need for me to be at home with them. God urged my wife to support me, but in a way that gently and subtly told me to consider putting family first when the next opportunity arose. Although many friends in Bravo Company wanted me to stay, God gave them understanding, helping them realize that mine was a family decision. They respected my decision and made me feel good about choosing to step down.

Now does this mean that my friends who chose to stay in the Army aren't devoted family men and women? Absolutely not! They are some of the most devoted and loving husbands, wives and parents that I know. I admire and applaud their commitment to family life. I firmly believe that God has asked them to stay in the military for His reasons, many of which are at work as I write these words. God certainly works in mysterious ways.

And so, what do I see as the Lord's purpose for my life? There are so many things I will never understand, and God's life plan for me is one of them. But as I go through life, I feel God's guiding hand directing me certain ways. Too many facets of my life have changed spiritually over the past year to ignore God's calling me to share my reflections with others. I feel called to write for the glory of our Creator's name. I feel compelled to tell family, friends and co-workers about God's amazing grace. Above all, I feel the pressing need to write to all who would read and tell them about the joy I have found in Christ. How fantastic it is to know that I am forgiven for my sins and have been promised eternal life. How awesome it is to know that one day I will join the multitudes of angels and saints in singing praises to the Lord.

When I find my life in turmoil, when I am faced with insurmountable challenges, God is there to wrap those tender, loving arms around me and give me peace. How important it is for me to share this with everybody I can while I am here on this earth.

As I write this book, many of my friends are living in the deserts of Iraq. They are enduring mid-day temperatures as high as 130° Fahrenheit and persistent sandstorms that create countless problems. I cannot begin to imagine how hard it must be to constantly have sand in everything…in your clothes, the bedding you sleep in, equipment, in your hair and eyes, and even in your food. All of these hardships are in addition to the daily threat on their very lives from enemy forces nearby.

Our soldiers are all too familiar with the "hurry up and wait" syndrome synonymous with military procedures. There are often times when soldiers are idle, waiting for orders or supplies. Where my friends are serving, they do not have the luxury of watching television or sitting in the easy chair. They have to spend their time in a hot, desolate country, thousands of miles away from loved ones and home. My heart goes out to each and every one of our soldiers who are so honorably serving America.

All too often, I hear people speak out against our nation for using military force in conflicts that could be settled peacefully. This conflict in Iraq is no exception. Many judgements are thrown around idly, as if we have the right to judge. Lest we forget, so many heroes have sacrificed their lives before us to allow us the freedoms we currently have and grasp onto so tightly.

My simple mind cannot fathom all that is taking place in our government and in our world. I could not possibly comprehend all the factors our government and President must weigh to make the decisions they do every day. And so I must put faith in our heavenly Lord.

I would ask you to pray with me. For my family of friends who are in the country of Iraq, and all others, serving our nation with honor and dignity, I ask that you join me in this prayer:

*Ron Puettmann*

Dear Lord,

Please stand by our soldiers who have given up their freedoms and have left homeland and families to faithfully serve You and this country. Bless and protect them as they honorably fulfill their duties half a world away from the ones they love. Many of us are able to continue our lives uninterrupted, not knowing the pain, anguish and hardship that these soldiers and their families must be going through. Please help us to give thanks and praise to You for sparing us from this trial and for the peace and safety we enjoy. Please bring our families and friends back to us safely, and in their service, may they find You, Your comfort and Your peace.

I would also pray that in their service, thousands more soldiers will enlist in Your holy army here on earth.

Amen.

✝

# Chapter 14

# Suggestion Box

**"O Lord, you are my God; I will exalt you and praise your name, for in perfect faithfulness you have done marvelous things, things planned long ago." (Isaiah 25:1)**

## Autumn Hikes

Make time to take a walk down an autumn trail, littered with fallen leaves of every shape and color. Let the leaves brush by the wayside as you meander under canopies of gold and crimson, blankets of yellows and reds. As sunbeams find their way through the leafy mazes above, open your mind and soul to wherever they may take you. Let your cares and concerns melt away as you enjoy tranquility seldom equaled in this fast-paced, busy world. As leaves fall carelessly to the ground around you, lift up praise to the Lord for creating such splendor.

159

Try making these walks spiritual times, opportunities to speak to God and tell Him what is on your heart and mind. Feel the Lord's presence surround you as you shuffle through a carpet of leaves amongst playful yet busy squirrels diligently preparing for another long, cold winter. Take your cares, your concerns, your fears, your hopes, your dreams…take them all to God in prayer. Our Lord is always there to listen.

## Gravel Roads

Venture off of the highway sometime down a gravel road and explore. Very few people take the time to stroll down gravel roads anymore. There is more nature around us than we can possibly experience, and it is closer than we may think. Some of the neatest natural and spiritual areas I have found have been along gravel roads, just off the beaten path.

# We all Wake up on the Wrong Side of the Bed Occasionally

Some days don't start out quite right. Once in a while it's a stubbed toe as you stumble downstairs in the dark. Maybe it's the craving for a certain bowl of cereal only to discover after you have poured the cereal into the bowl that you're out of milk. Perhaps you're running late for work when you hop in the car, turn the ignition and nothing happens. Whatever the case, you have started your day out on the wrong foot. How do you turn it around? Try starting it with a prayer. Even as you sit at the edge of your bed in that half-awake state, knowing you have to get up but wishing you could lay back down, say the Lord's prayer. Ask God to grant you strength and endurance on this day. Then, as your day progresses when something goes wrong, first and foremost, send it to God in prayer. The Lord will help you through all of the turmoil, all of the stress, all of the hardship. God can calm your soul and instantly send you His peace.

# Be Fair to God

Take serious time to consider your level of giving to God. Also consider what things in life you spend your money on that you don't need. Maybe you are careful not to spend money on unnecessary things. Perhaps every penny you earn goes towards providing for your family. God knows. God knows everything.

Take a serious look at how you spend your extra time. Are you being a servant for God? Are you taking time to help the church, help the less fortunate, and help your neighbor? Maybe you have no extra time. Maybe you spend time away from work entirely with your family. God knows. God knows everything.

Remember that everything we have belongs to God, and is a gift given to us by God. Storing up earthly rewards is something each of us does. How much more important it is to focus on storing up *heavenly* rewards.

# Get Rid of the Stress

Take a look at the areas of your life that are causing you stress. Perhaps everything in your life causes stress, or perhaps there are only certain times of the day that challenge your patience. These may likely be times when you are driving in your car or when you are spending time at work. Whatever the case, identify those areas now, and find "improving grounds."

If driving to and from work is the culprit, make a few changes. Start ten minutes earlier in the morning so you can become less frustrated by red lights and slower drivers. Force yourself to travel at the *real* speed limit. This differs from the imaginary speed limit (that speed limit where people feel they can safely travel without getting pulled over by an officer, usually between 5 and 10 mph over the *real* speed limit). Give the person ahead of you a four-second gap. Instead of riding their bumper, stay back a fair distance.

Another method you can try if you have a tachometer (the meter that shows your RPM) in your vehicle is to keep it under 2500 rpm all of the time. Most vehicles when driven at 65 mph on the interstate run somewhere around 2000 rpm. When I thought of this, I immediately tried it. It amazed me how many times I would normally have gone over. Yet staying under it felt pretty good. My car probably thanked me too, as I wasn't abusing the accelerator so much.

If you rely on coffee to get you through the day, drink half as much and pray twice as much! Ask the Lord for strength and endurance to sustain you. God will not let you down.

If co-worker or supervisor conflicts are causing stress, ask the Lord prayerfully that His will for you would be revealed in that place (please remember that God hears all prayers and answers them in His time, not ours). As you await the Lord's answer, pray for those who make your life stressful. Ask yourself if there are ways you can serve these individuals as a Christian.

When one comes to know and accept God's promise and the heavenly path of righteousness, the stress will diminish as your attitude and perspective changes to focus on the teachings of Christ. The joy and peace of God's love counterbalances and grossly outweighs the negative burdens of this world.

As you can probably tell, there are many small ways we can adjust our lives to reduce stress. Contrary to popular belief, people *are* capable of change. Everything is possible with God.

If you're at the rope's end with stress in your life, turn your life over completely to God. Ask God for peace. Our saving Lord will not forsake you.

Having a child in school, I often think about what public school teachers must see and hear. I'm certain it is often quite revealing how children are treated at home by their behavior at school. Children can be a source of stress, but I think some of this is parent-induced. In order to eliminate this stress, parents must first pray for the Lord's guidance in regards to raising their children. Ask God to intervene in your relationship and give you patience. Request that you may give your children the unconditional love that God gives you. Consider how you treat your children when your patience has run out. Do you yell, throw things, or discipline out of anger? Children need to feel loved, in order to grow into loving people as they mature. We as parents need to provide this love at all times in the relationships we have with our children.

# Get Away

If you have never done so, make some time for yourself to spend with the Lord. Make time in your busy schedule and busy life to reflect on your faith journey and your relationship with Christ. Retreats are very rewarding and restful for the soul. If you have not spent a day or weekend in fellowship with other Christians, learning and talking about God, I encourage you to do so and experience the fantastic ways that our Lord and the Holy Spirit can move your heart.

# Read the Bible

Have you ever experienced moments in your life where you wished you could just open up a manual and find out how to fix what was hurting or broken? The bible is that book. It is an operator's manual for our lives. It is an instruction manual, giving us guidance on how to treat others and ourselves. It contains God's authority on finances, marriage, friendships, work, relationships and all sorts of topics we deal with on a daily basis.

In my opinion, the bible should not collect dust on a shelf. It should be read every day. We should not leave it up to those in ministry to teach us everything in the bible.

If you have not done so, open it up and start reading. Start with the new testament and the books of Matthew, Mark, Luke and John. Learn more about the life of Jesus, and then dive deeper into the works of the apostles, the disciples and the prophets.

If you do read the bible regularly, consider attending a bible study program. It is a fantastic way to discuss scripture with others and find deeper meaning in God's word.

✝

# Chapter 15

# Prayer

**"Within your temple, O God, we meditate on your unfailing love." (Psalm 48:9)**

One sunny afternoon, I was driving down the interstate. I turned the radio off and said a prayer to God. I began praying for my family, my friends, for peace in our country and world, for the military who is overseas protecting our country. Before long, one short prayer became many combined prayers. I prayed for our soldiers and the leaders of this great nation, that they may make wise decisions and that they will bring honor to God's holy name. I prayed for all of the families and friends who remained at home, trying to cope with life in a troubled country and a world filled with turmoil. I prayed for the children who are without their moms, dads, or both, and search for understanding. I prayed for compassion, that God may see in our hearts true remorse for suffering and true gratefulness for the sacrifices of our soldiers. As my heart opened up to the realities of war, I prayed for the innocent bystanders. I prayed for those who were left homeless and hungry, those in need of medical aid, those who had lost loved ones. One thing led to another and soon I was praying for many of the great tragedies of this world: disease and hunger, sickness and death, homelessness and famine, hatred and discrimination, poverty, terrorism and even war. I said many different prayers that afternoon, many more than I had originally intended to say. But I let God take the lead, and He opened my heart. God helped me realize that there are so many people in need of our Lord's divine help. More times than not, I have turned my back on these problems and have been blind to those in need. When I realize my selfishness, I ask the Lord for forgiveness and grace, so that with each new day, I may be more attentive and responsive to the needs of others.

After fifteen minutes of specific prayers, I had to say, "Dear God, if I could narrow my prayers down today, I would ask that You help me to understand Your will in my life. Please help me to accept Your will and to serve You, first and foremost, every day."

There are so many things to pray for. I feel that praying for wisdom to make the right choices and asking for understanding to accept the plans God has for our lives are two great places to begin in our daily worship to the Lord.

One thing I have learned in my lifetime is that God is in complete control. I take great comfort in knowing this. Our Almighty God is so much bigger than any hardships or difficulties I may encounter in my daily life. All I need to do to alleviate the fear, anxiety and the stresses of life is to pray.

Talk with God each day, like He is right there beside you. Take every concern, every problem, and every need to our heavenly Father. In addition, give thanks for every good thing under the sun.

What follows in this chapter are several prayers I have prayed, short conversations I have had with our Lord when I have needed encouragement, asked for hope, or simply wanted to give thanks.

One prayer I have said daily for over fifteen years helps me to open my heart before I start each busy day.

Dear Lord,

Please bless me this day.

Give me the grace that I need.

Come into my life. Amen.

By saying this each day, I ask God for three things: 1) That the Lord would give me guidance and direction by blessing the way I treat others, the way I speak and the things I do; 2) That God would grant me forgiveness for my sins and weaknesses, yet grant me hope that I can change and make straight my path; and 3) That the Lord would be at the center of every thought, every word and every action of mine.

I have hope that these prayers will be encouraging to you. Talking with God encourages me each day, and it is a wonderful feeling to have a God who will listen to every single thing we say. It is so comforting to have a God who makes time for us, even when we forget to make time for Him.

One afternoon among oak trees and the sounds of a cardinal's song, I jotted down the following phrase. It sums up life pretty well in my mind. I have made it my personal motto, one I can refer to at the end of each day to see if I have spent my day as a Christian.

"In the end, the two things that matter most are that you've treated your neighbor like yourself, and that you've put your life in the hands of the Lord."

Dear Lord,

There are blessed mornings when Your heavenly light shines through the tree branches and across frost-covered fields. I can see the almighty power You hold. Dear God, shine Your most glorious light on us. Help us to see Your light not only with our eyes, but also with our hearts. Help us to realize the joy and peace that You offer and give us the strength and grace to carry Your light to others. Amen.

Dear Lord,

There are days when I find life challenging. No matter what I do, it is hard to motivate myself physically, mentally, emotionally, even spiritually. Days like this make heaven seem eternally distant. O gracious Savior, grant me Your grace. Help me to realize that even on the toughest of days, nothing I do can compare to the death Your Son endured on the cross. Please allow the memory of His sacrifice to be a beacon of uplifting strength and endurance to me as I seek to do Your will each day. Amen.


Dear Lord,

Often times in my life I get anxious. It may be from driving on icy roads, awaiting an important job interview or preparing for a speech. Lord, when I allow that uncomfortable feeling to take over, it gnaws away at me like a terrible disease. Heavenly Lord, help me to set aside the apprehension, the nervousness and the anxiety in my life. Help me to realize that you have control of my life, right down to the last heartbeat.

Help me to approach each anxious situation with the understanding that Your will is above all. Give me the grace to embrace Your will, no matter what the outcome. And if I may ask so much dear Lord, may Your will draw me closer to You. Amen.

Dear Lord,

Sometimes my life goes by so fast, I take for granted all of your countless blessings. From the moment I awaken each morning until the moment I retire each evening, more blessing are given to me than I could possibly ever imagine.

Help me O Lord to take a few steps back. Reveal to me Your handiwork in the nature and people around me. Allow my senses to fully appreciate all of life this day, and may I continue to praise and glorify You daily with renewed awareness and gratefulness. Amen.

Dear Lord,

Please give me a thankful heart. Help me to realize the multitude of blessings you have bestowed upon me. Each moment of the day, the temple You created in me is at work. I take it for granted all too often.

From my very heartbeat and the air I breathe, to hearing Your creation all around me, Your wondrous gifts are countless. I am able to see millions of things each day. I am able to talk, sing and whisper. I can feel so many different things with only the slightest touch of my hand. The list for each of us in this world is endless, dear Lord.

Help me to recognize all of Your blessings and give thanks for them, lest they be taken away from me. Help me also Lord to use each of these blessings to further Your holy name. Amen.


Dear Lord,

Often I find myself thinking about heaven and what it must be like to be there worshipping You among all of Your angels. Since the dawn of mankind, You have gathered literally billions of souls who are spending eternity serving You as angels. I can only imagine how beautiful the harmony when your heavenly choir sings! As much as I long to be there with You, worshipping and singing praise, help me to realize that there is work to be done here on earth. You have put me here to fulfill Your purpose. Guide me each day with your loving grace, and give me understanding that I may recognize and make those choices that will lead me toward Your heavenly throne. Amen.

*Ron Puettmann*

Dear Lord,

As I awaken each morning, help me to realize that I need to live my life for You. Help me to focus on building my day around serving You and expanding Your kingdom. In all that I do, in all that I say, in all that I think, give me grace, that I may strive to be more like Your perfect Son, Jesus Christ. Amen.

Dear Lord,

There are so many times when fear seizes me, when anxiety grabs my shoulders and shakes me to no end. Send down Your loving grace, O Lord. Remind me that You are in control. Give me strength to cast off the burdens that weigh down my life, and help me to lift these burdens up to You. Amen.

Dear Lord,

I believe that You have created me for Your higher purpose. I believe that someday, You will ask me to give praise to You in such a way that my praises will reach countless eyes and ears. When this day comes, please give me the courage to let the floodgates open and pour forth blessings and words of spiritual encouragement that I never knew were in me. I pray that I will not hide in fear or shame, or hold my tongue when my heart says to speak. Rather, I ask for Your courage, that I will glorify You and bring honor to Your holy name. Amen.

Dear Lord,

You have granted me more blessings than I deserve or am worthy of. Each day I reflect on the abundance of peace and joy You have brought into my life. Please help me on this day to give my gift back to You. Help me to be Christian in my thoughts, words, and actions, and help me to be the kind of person You would have me be. For I trust entirely in Your saving grace and give thanks and praise to Your holy name. Amen

Dear Lord,

Please stand beside me today, O Lord. Give my life guidance through Your holy direction. Grant me the peace of Your constant grace. Hold me close to You, and fill my heart with Your boundless love. May my daily prayers and supplications reflect devotion and loyalty to the one true living God. Amen

Dear Lord,

Thank you for allowing me to wake this morning. Come rain or shine, You have given me the promise of a new day, and for this I am truly thankful. Help me to fully grasp the potential that You have placed in front of me today. Help me to show my love for You by serving others. Amen.

Dear Lord,

As I awaken each day, I face uncertainty in my life. Not knowing what lies ahead in my future makes me anxious. Sometimes I get anxious because I know what events are going to take place, and I am scared. Some days I get so concerned wondering whether my family will stay safe and healthy, what kind of day I will have, or whether I can accomplish the goals I set for myself. Sometimes I anxiously ponder if today is the day that You will call my name.

Lord, help me to understand that Your will is supreme. Free me from the chains of anxiety. Calm my soul with

Your peace and comfort. Allow Your peace to flow through me as I sit on the bank of Your holy river, my feet dipped into cool, soothing waters. Free my mind from earthly concerns, and fill my heart with prayer and praise unto You. Amen.

Dear Lord,

It is so reassuring to know that in a world filled with pain and suffering, you are our constant companion, our most holy Comforter. With gentle and unending love, You wrap Your arms around us in our darkest hours. Thank You for Your faithfulness in loving us. May we constantly seek to return Your gift by following Your example and comforting those around us. Amen.

# † 

# Conclusion

**"And anyone who does not carry his cross and follow me cannot be my disciple." (Luke 14:27)**

I have a long way to go in my faith journey. God knows that I am human and imperfect. I make mistakes, I don't listen well at times, and yet at other times, I fail to serve, as Christ would have me serve. Yet, as a Christian, I know that God's love is unfailing. I know that Jesus Christ died on a cross for my sins. And I have felt the Lord pick me up and encourage me at those times where my own human weakness and inadequacy prevented me from doing His will. God's unending grace keeps me striving even harder to carry the Christian message to others and treat others with respect and brotherly love.

I have to thank God for growing up in such a loving family. Mom and dad have been the greatest, most giving parents in the world, loving, guiding and encouraging me all of my life. My five brothers (Steve, Gary, Phil, Brian and Ray) and five sisters (Linda, Kathy, Deb, Janet and Judy) motivated, inspired, encouraged and loved me all of these years. I am grateful to each of them for their part in shaping my life (and putting up with me!).

As I wrote this book, a thought came forth that truly made me smile. By writing down words from my heart and having them published for others to read, the potential exists for these words to reach more people than I could ever meet and talk with in my lifetime. Granted, we're talking potential here, but just the thought of it makes me smile. What makes my heart sing with rejoice is the thought of bringing somebody closer to our heavenly Lord.

So whether it is in the forest, at the kitchen table, or worshiping with your church family, open your heart to the will of God and be ready to follow wherever the Holy Spirit will lead you.

May God bless you on your faith journey.


**"...'No eye has seen, no ear has heard, no mind has conceived what God has prepared for those who love him.'" (1 Corinthians 2:9) †**

*Ron Puettmann*

## About the Author

Ron Puettmann lives near Solon in eastern Iowa with his wife, Karla and two sons, Tyler and Kyle. Growing up on a farm in northern Iowa, Ron has long enjoyed the peace and tranquility of life in a rural setting. He is blessed to work at Lake Macbride, one of Iowa's largest and most beautiful state parks.

A 1995 graduate of Iowa State University, Puettmann holds a Bachelor's of Science Degree in Fisheries and Wildlife Biology and a specialization in Interpretation of Natural Resources.

Ron loves the outdoors, and finds writing an exciting way to express his passions for God and nature. You are sure to find this passion unfold in his first book, *Faith and Forest*.

Printed in the United States
1491900006B/147